# JESUS AND THE LIVING PAST

# JESUS
## AND THE LIVING PAST

### THE HALE LECTURES 1978

## MICHAEL RAMSEY

Oxford    New York    Toronto    Melbourne

OXFORD UNIVERSITY PRESS

1980

*Oxford University Press, Walton Street, Oxford* OX2 6DP

OXFORD LONDON GLASGOW
NEW YORK TORONTO MELBOURNE WELLINGTON
KUALA LUMPUR SINGAPORE JAKARTA HONG KONG TOKYO
DELHI BOMBAY CALCUTTA MADRAS KARACHI
NAIROBI DAR ES SALAAM CAPE TOWN

*British Library Cataloguing in Publication Data*

*Ramsey, Arthur Michael*
*Jesus and the living past.*
*1. Jesus Christ*
*I. Title*
232    *BT202*    *79-42864*

*ISBN 0-19-213963-0*

Printed in Great Britain by
Richard Clay (The Chaucer Press), Ltd.,
Bungay, Suffolk

# PREFACE

This book contains the Hale Lectures given at Seabury-Western Theological Seminary in Evanston in the fall of 1978. It was my privilege to be the Hale lecturer for the second time, my first series having been given in 1959 with the title *From Gore to Temple: an Era in Anglican Theology*. I am grateful to the Hale Trustees and to Dean O. C. Edwards for this renewed confidence and kindness after twenty years.

The former series had been concerned with the history of a theological era which ended forty years ago with the beginning of the Second World War. The subsequent years have been years of confusion in theology as in much else in the world, and a fair appraisal of both the creative and the negative factors must await a longer perspective of history. These lectures discuss some of the questions which have become prominent, and it is my hope that readers of this book may be helped in their thinking about what is passing and what is lasting in Christian belief and experience. While theology includes a variety of academic disciplines and demands rigorous intellectual integrity it is, I believe, properly inseparable from the knowledge of God through prayer and contemplation and the Christian life.

Besides the Hale Lectures this work includes a lecture on Christian Sacrifice given at Huron College, Ontario, in the spring of 1976; and some of the material in this book was used in the Hensley Henson Lectures given in Oxford in 1977 with the title 'History and Contemporary Christianity'.

My thanks go to Mrs. Margaret Parkinson for her great help in the typing of the work.

Durham
Easter 1979

MICHAEL RAMSEY

# CONTENTS

# Chapter One

# THE CHRISTIAN STORY

## I

Christianity has long been described as a historical religion. It has its centre in the life, death and resurrection of Jesus in the land of Palestine at the time when Pontius Pilate was governor of Judea. Christians believe that in these events God revealed himself to mankind in a unique way and accomplished something upon which the salvation of the world depends. Christianity has furthermore been dominated and defined not only by the events but by the person who is their subject: Jesus. Because of the belief in the resurrection of Jesus after his death by crucifixion, the person of Jesus has been held to belong not only to the past but to the present for Christians in every epoch. One of the New Testament writers, the author of the Epistle to the Hebrews, says in an abrupt ejaculation, 'Jesus Christ [is] the same yesterday and today and for ever' (Hebrews 13: 8). The words include no verb and are an outburst rather than a sentence, affirming the Christian conviction that Jesus somehow transcends the distances of time.

This historical character seems to affect every aspect of Christianity. Its concept of God is deeply bound up with the event and words of Jesus. Its worship is filled with thanksgiving for what that event accomplished. The Christian life is seen as a response in gratitude and dependence towards what God did for mankind in Jesus; 'We love because he first loved us' (1 John 4: 19), 'the life I now live in the flesh I live by faith in the Son of God, who loved me and gave himself for me' (Galatians 2: 20). The calling of a Christian is to grow up into the apprehension of Jesus and into his likeness, a calling described as sharing in his death and resurrection. These are some of the inherent characteristics of Christianity as a historical religion.

The varieties of thought and doctrine in the Christian centuries have seemed to emphasize this historical character. Reformations and movements of renewal have appealed to some aspect of Jesus or the apostolic teaching about him as the biblical records witness to him, and the various revolutions in Christian theology have been eager to claim that history is on their side. Thus the Liberal Protestantism of the last century rejected the traditional orthodox dogma by making an appeal to the history of Jesus before and behind the theology of the early Church, sure that this history was discoverable. More recently Rudolf Bultmann and his disciples have argued that we can know next to nothing about the history of Jesus before the crucifixion, and have urged that the basis of Christianity is in the existential 'faith event' of the death of Jesus preached and believed. This presentation, while it is sceptical about a great deal of the historical tradition, affirms for Christianity a historical particularity no less than other species of Christian thought. Christianity as a historical religion has through the centuries had its devoted adherents as well as those who have rejected it, whether through incredulity or apathy or adherence to some other allegiance. The word 'scandal' has often been prominent. To the critics it has seemed scandalous that an infinite and eternal deity should give exclusive prominence to a single set of happenings in one short time and in one small place. To Christians it has often been acceptable that theirs is a scandalous religion likely to evoke either faith or ridicule.

Today however the nature of Christianity as a historical faith is being questioned not only by critics beyond its frontiers but by some thoughtful minds within the orbit of those who profess, or desire to profess, allegiance to Christianity. Some of the questionings arise from trends in the study of the nature of history which go back some way, while some of them belong more directly to what may be called the contemporary climate of thought. It seems fair to say that four kinds of question are specially prominent.

Is our knowledge of the history of Jesus secure enough to bear the weight which Christianity puts upon it? There are those who, sceptical about much of the historical tradition concerning Jesus, would wish to appeal less to any known facts about him than to the impact of Jesus upon the first believers and their successors; this is still an appeal to history albeit of an indirect kind. There are also those whose historical scepticism leads them to look in directions other than those of history for the maintenance of some form of Christianity. There are those who look to the Christian tradition as a broad phenomenon while being very uncertain of its historical origins.

It is also asked whether the early Church drew the right inferences from the original gospel in affirming the doctrine that Jesus is divine and God incarnate. Is the belief that Jesus is the Word made flesh a necessary understanding of the primitive gospel, or is it an arbitrary or dispensable development or 'model'?

Then it is asked whether religious concepts are not intelligible only within a particular cultural setting and cannot be presented in other cultural settings without either a historical irrelevance or such modernizing as distorts identity. Phrases which have become prominent are 'the pastness of the past' and 'cultural relativity'. The questions are real ones, as it is possible to present Jesus so much as the Jew of first century Palestine that his relevance today is hard to see, or to present him so paraphrased and modernized as to raise doubts about it being the real Jesus who is presented.

It is also asked by not a few whether the particularity of divine revelation in Jesus, in terms of time and place and culture and religion, is compatible with a right appreciation of the divine action in the world and in history as a whole, as well as in the other great religions which have come increasingly to be more involved with one another.

It is with these questions that this book will be concerned, and I would say a little about the method which will be followed and some of the presuppositions which will be in evidence.

First, this book is written by one who believes that historical criticism must be used honestly and rigorously in the study of the biblical writings and the origins of Christianity. He differs from those who would invoke a doctrine of inspiration in the interests of the literal historical character of the records, for divine inspiration (in which he whole-heartedly believes) can belong to poetry, drama, symbol, interpretation as well as to factual chronicles. But the use of critical science includes a willingness to criticize some of the assumptions which can be used in its pursuit.

Second, it is my belief that the understanding both of the history and the theology of Christianity cannot properly be separated from the study of Christian spirituality. What is the character of the Christian life? What is the nature of Christian saintliness? How far is it linked with a response to the historical givenness of the gospel, or to the divine self-giving in history? These are questions of supreme significance, and a good deal of contemporary discussion ignores them.

Third, theories about the pastness of the past and about cultural relativity cannot properly be understood within the orbit of academic study and discipline alone. As one who has through half a century tried to present the Christian faith in a variety of settings in the contemporary world, I believe, through my own inadequacies, that the contemporary experience of the preacher, the pastor, the apologist, the spiritual guide, matters no less than academic disciplines for the understanding of what is possible and not possible in the presentation of an ancient faith in a modern setting.

The relation between the past and the present has taken a variety of forms in the course of human experience. There have been communities whose mental outlook has been deeply affected by the collective memory of past events, so that we sometimes speak of people as living in the past. There have also been communities to whom the past has been a creative source of vitality and change. We speak also of a dead past as one which has lost influence and relevance, and of a living past as one whose impact is so vivid that past and present seem to be mingled. Paradoxically a living past may sometimes have a deadening effect by dampening the fire of contemporary creativity. It is in a world full of these varied kinds of experience that we study the relation of Christianity and history.

In the first age of Christianity, apostolic writers show a keen sense of a past that is living, and living in such a way as to evoke new understandings and energies in the various cultural settings into which Christianity moved.

## II

The earliest Christian preaching had the death and resurrection of Jesus at the centre. The belief in the resurrection included both the action of God in raising Jesus from the dead and the contemporary presence of Jesus as alive. This did not mean however that the crucifixion of Jesus belonged to the past alone, for it was continually emphasized that the Jesus who is alive and contemporary is the Jesus who was once crucified. 'To have been crucified' was an ever-present aspect of Jesus, and the crucifixion continued to be seen as a timeless confrontation between the judgement and compassion of God and the sinfulness of the human race. Both Baptism and the Eucharist emphasized the continuing significance of the death of Jesus. In Baptism converts were believed to be united with Jesus in his death, and the Eucharist was a showing forth of his death and a recalling of his death into the present time.

Moreover, the idea of a living past included not only the events of the gospel but the story of Israel as it was presented in the scriptures of the old covenant. The apostles found that as a result of the fulfilment by Jesus of the hopes and promises of Israel, these scriptures came alive in a new way as now telling of Jesus. This is apparent in a variety of ways. There is the use of Old Testament proof-texts in many of the New Testament writings. There is the belief that themes of the Old Testament, such as the exodus, the covenant, the presence, the temple, the people of God, are fulfilled in Jesus and appear in a new and exalted way. There is also the belief that the broad sweep of revelation in the Old Testament is gathered up and fulfilled in the events of Jesus, as when St. Luke's Gospel describes Jesus, on the road to Emmaus, as interpreting to two bewildered disciples the scriptures concerning himself (Luke 24: 27). The Ethiopian eunuch was, in an episode in the Acts of the Apostles, reading the fifty-third chapter of Isaiah, and Philip the evangelist tells him that it is about Jesus that he is reading (Acts 8: 28–35).

The concept of the living past is emphasized for the early Christians by their belief in the rôle of the Holy Spirit. In St. Paul's teaching the Spirit is emphatically the spirit of the risen Jesus, and the lively presence of the Holy Spirit in the Christians has the effect of building them up into the life of the body of Christ, a life continually related to his death and resurrection. By the presence of the Holy Spirit the impact of the death and resurrection of Jesus continues. This work of the Holy Spirit to which the Epistles give widespread testimony, is specially emphasized in the supper discourse in the Fourth Gospel. Here it is taught that it is the rôle of the Holy Spirit to witness to Jesus, to enable the disciples to witness, to recall to their minds the things that Jesus said, and to convict the world concerning its attitude to Jesus and his death. This activity is summed up by saying that the Spirit will take the things of Jesus and declare them to the disciples, and that the Spirit will glorify Jesus in the lives of the disciples. Amidst the new modes of interpretation in the Fourth Gospel the emphasis upon the living past is powerfully continued.

So the apostolic writings show how powerful is the idea of the living past, and with it there is linked the Christian hope concerning the future. The hope for the future has its root in the Christian faith in what God has done in the coming of Jesus. There is thus the certain hope that what God has begun in the story of Israel, in the death and resurrection of the Messiah, in the presence of the Holy Spirit, will find completion in the final vindication of God's purpose. The eschatological expectation has, in the apostolic age, a variety of forms, but all of them seem to be grounded in the living past. Thus there is in the earlier letters of St. Paul the hope of the return of Jesus in glory.

There is the hope of the coming of the Kingdom of God, a hope made sure by the revelation of divine sovereignty in Jesus. There is the hope of a final vision of Jesus himself as the climax of the Christians' present possession of eternal life in union with him. While the variety of pictures of the Christian hope show its connection with the past and the present, no passage perhaps shows this more vividly than the eighth chapter of the Epistle to the Romans, where the present activity of the Holy Spirit and the apostle's faith in the divine sovereignty in face of the world's calamities and frustrations anticipate the goal of future glory.

Past, present, future. Nowhere more than in the Eucharist is this unity apparent. In the eucharistic rite the death of the Lord is recalled into the present while the Christians feed upon the living Jesus who is the bread of heaven, and anticipate the future in the prayer: Lord, come.

It can therefore be hardly gainsaid that in the Christianity of the apostolic age there is a faith in the living past such as determines the hope for the future, and this faith is linked with the experience of a Christ who is believed to belong to past, present, and future alike.

Through the centuries the living past has been realized in Christian experience, for it is the work of the Holy Spirit to reproduce it in its dynamic power. But it has been all too easy for the perversity of Christians to twist it into being a past that can be even deadening rather than creative. It is possible to have a devotion to the Bible as the inspired document of Christianity and yet to miss the dynamic work of the Holy Spirit in bringing its message home to the conscience and the imagination in a particular age. It is possible to have a devotion to the words of the Creeds and other definitions, which misses the sense of mystery which belongs to all religious language. It is possible to adhere to the truth that is in Jesus in such a way as to miss the energy of the Spirit in leading the believers along the way of deepening apprehension of that truth. It is possible to cling to particular aspects of the apostolic experience and language so as to miss the larger context in which these aspects are a part. It is possible also to ignore the work of the divine *logos* in the world beyond the Christian covenant, for that work can help in the understanding of the particular revelation in Christ. It is equally possible to be so obsessed by passing trends as to miss the longer perspective of truth. In all these ways the devotion of Christians to the past may miss the dynamism of its living character.

Yet the perversity of Christians, which is as old as the apostolic age, as indeed St. Paul's dealings with the Church of Corinth show, does not prevent the witness of the Holy Spirit to the living past. By saintly Christian lives, by worship and spirituality, by preaching and teaching, by a hundred ways of imaginative creativity and practical service, the living past is made known. It has kept alive the hope both of heaven and of the Kingdom of God on earth, and it has enabled the transfiguring of human lives already in the midst of sorrow and suffering. But the heart of the matter has been the Christian story. May we think a little about its character?

## III

The Christian story was told in the apostolic age in a variety of ways.

First, there was the story of the crucifixion and the resurrection of Jesus preached by the apostles. St. Paul preached in Corinth that Jesus had died and was buried and was raised on the third day and appeared to the apostles and others, and he says that this was a tradition which he had received (1 Corinthians 15: 3–5). The death and the resurrection were two parts of one story. But the death had been so vindicated as itself a mighty piece of good news that it was possible to tell of the death itself as a powerful story: 'the word of the cross' (1 Corinthians 1: 18), 'we preach Christ crucified' (1 Corinthians 1: 23). The story of the cross could indeed be vivid in the telling, and to the people in Galatia 'Jesus Christ was publicly portrayed as crucified' (Galatians 3: 1).

The story of the death and the resurrection was in no vacuum. Speeches in the Acts of the Apostles in particular show the story to be of one piece with the prophecy in the Old Testament which prepared the way, and with the subsequent mission of the Holy Spirit and indeed the coming return of Jesus in glory.

Next, there were the stories about deeds and words of Jesus, told in the oral tradition within the Christian communities. These stories form the background to much of the narrative in the Synoptic Gospels. Sometimes it is a mighty work of Jesus, sometimes a saying, which is the centre of the particular story. While the stories are about Jesus in the days of his ministry before the crucifixion, they would be told in the Christian communities with the awareness of Jesus as alive and contemporary, and the Easter faith would no doubt colour the form and the telling of the story.

Eventually, there came the written Gospels. Each author tells the Christian story with his own aim, range and portraiture. Mark's Gospel begins with the preaching of John the Baptist and the baptism of Jesus in Jordan, and it ends with the women running in awe and bewilderment from the tomb.[1] It is not a 'life of Jesus', but rather the story of how Jesus the Son of God proclaimed the

Kingdom of God and in the serving of God's purpose suffered and died, with the promise of vindication beyond his death. Matthew's Gospel begins with the birth of Jesus and ends with the risen Jesus enjoining the disciples to carry to all nations the message of the new righteousness. Jesus is presented as the royal Messiah, teaching the righteousness of the kingdom of heaven for the new community and giving warning of future judgement. Luke's story begins with an expectant company in Israel and tells of the birth of Jesus as the beginning of salvation, and the story continues beyond the exodus of Jesus to death and to glory into a second volume telling of the carrying of the gospel to the nations. The story conveys the continuing sweep of history with a wonderful sensitivity to Jewish origins and to Gentile outreach.

Within the synoptic tradition, presented by the three evangelists in different ways, two 'modes' of story are present. One is the mode of down-to-earth story-telling, as of happenings within the scrutiny of eyewitness and evidence; and the other is the mode of a story of what God is doing, a kind of story beyond historical categories. Lastly, the Gospel of John tells the story of how God revealed his glory in the life and death and resurrection of Jesus. But if in John's Gospel the mode of a divine story is most explicit, so is a powerful emphasis upon historical fact as a necessary part of the divine salvation. The 'flesh' of Jesus, and the 'flesh' of history, are a vital part of the theme.

It is at once the stumbling-block and the glory of Christianity that a story of facts which history can investigate and a story of God's action in the events are interwoven. This interweaving involves questions about language. Perhaps an imaginary incident may help in our consideration of these questions. Suppose that during one of my lectures an angel came and sat on one of the seats and joined in our discussion of these questions, would that be history? We would need to be sure of the sobriety of our witnesses, but if an obviously non-human figure did appear in this way it would certainly be history, for history is no less history if an event is unprecedented or extraordinary. But suppose someone went on to say that the angel had come down from heaven and returned to heaven after enjoying the lecture, that would not be history, for historical science knows nothing of the relation of heaven and earth. It might be utterly true as a statement of the angel's relation to God, but it would not be a mode of truth accessible to historical science. We could call the statement about the angel coming from heaven a symbolic or mythological statement so long as we were agreed about the use of language.

How does this definition of modes of language bear upon the Christian story? To say that Jesus lived and died and was alive again after death is to propound history, and if some of the happenings were unprecedented or supernatural they would none the less belong to history if they were within the range of observation and evidence. But to say that Jesus came down from heaven, or that he sits at the right hand of God, or that in Jesus God was made man, is to use language not in a historical mode but in a mode that we can call symbolic or mythological if the terms be agreed. The impression made by Jesus upon the early Church was such that they used the language of God sending and coming and giving to express their conviction that Jesus was and is divine.

A host of questions of course arise, and this book will be concerned with some of them. Was the divine story by which the event of Jesus was interpreted a wrong or arbitrary or dispensable factor, or was it a true interpretation? Meanwhile it has been the Christian story which has effectively carried Christianity to the imagination and conscience of thousands in every age and in many cultural settings. Within the story two scenes have always been prominent, the scene of the death of Jesus on the hill of Calvary and the scene of the birth at Bethlehem. Both these scenes have made their impact because of the divine dimension which they are believed to convey. The death of Jesus is felt to be not just one more in the series of the world's martyrdoms but the confrontation between God's judgement and compassion and the sin and suffering of mankind. So too the scene of the birth of Jesus has been felt to be not just the birthday of a wonderful person but the infinite and eternal God humbling himself in self-giving to the human race. If the understanding of the death and the birth of Jesus were otherwise, would Christianity be what it is?

## Chapter Two

# THE PASTNESS OF THE PAST?

Is it possible for us who live within the culture of the twentieth century to enter into the outlook of the New Testament writers who lived in a totally different culture, and to return with a message which is both their message and one which will be intelligible to our own contemporaries? It is certainly not easy, and those of us who try to fulfil this task are exposed to two perils. One is the peril of presenting a biblical message in its own categories in such a way that it will fail to reach many of our contemporaries. The other is the peril of producing a version of the biblical teaching so modernized that it is not essentially the same message as that of the apostles.

The problem has been discussed in some recent writings of Dr. Nineham: his Ethel M. Wood lecture in the University of London entitled *New Testament Interpretation in a Historical Age* and his book *The Use and Abuse of the Bible*, both published in 1976. Nineham poses the problem thus:

For every individual, no matter how original, to be a human being is to be to a large extent controlled by the ideas of the cultural community to which it is his destiny to belong. Furthermore, each cultural grouping has its own dominant ideas treated as absolutely valid and as part of the essentially human context. All this therefore poses problems for a religion which like Christianity claims that supernatural truth is revealed once for all in a particular life and teaching set in the context of a time, a culture and a community.[1]

Because this is so it is doubtful, Nineham argues, whether theological statements can convey meaning outside their own cultural setting, a doubt expressed in the phrase 'cultural relativity'. In any case the interpreter of the message of the Bible has an extremely difficult task. It is for him to make a mental journey into the past and absorb a set of ideas far removed from his own, and then to return to the contemporary world bringing what message he can from the ancient scene. So difficult is this that some of the most eminent interpreters have achieved little more than to simplify the Biblical message by reading modern patterns of thought into it. Describing some of these writers Nineham says:

For all their good intentions, Christian interpreters of the New Testament, because they believe themselves to be faced with a two-fold task, have tried to face all the ways, have faltered between two opinions. They have been aware of the peril of modernizing Jesus and the early Church, yet they have been loth to search them out in their full particularity and pastness with fear that in that form they would not speak directly to our condition. Thus they have interpreted New Testament accounts of the past as if they had been written by men who shared our attitude to the past; they have attributed to Jesus that essentially modern hybrid, 'realized eschatology'; they have read New Testament teaching on sacrifice, the wrath of God and the rest as if they had been produced by men who shared our understanding of the Old Testament, the nature and demands of God and much else beside. They have discovered in the New Testament a degree of unity or homogeneity it does not possess. The result is that the Jesus, the Paul, the Mark, the John of these interpreters and commentaries have been what Professor Trilling calls them, 'monstrous' figures that never were on land or sea. Schweitzer rightly pointed out that the truly historical Jesus was bound to be 'to our time a stranger and an enigma', incapable of being made symbolic and intelligible to the multitude by popular historical treatment. Could that language by used of the founder of Christianity as pictured by C. H.

Dodd, or of the existentialist Jesus of Bultmann and his followers, with his very twentieth century refusal to furnish any credentials or to make any Messianic claims? Are not these woefully hybrid figures precisely the products of reading of ancient texts through modern spectacles?[1]

I think that Nineham's analysis contains some fallacies which add to the difficulties he is describing.

First, is it possible that great teaching can have a power of reaching across the frontiers of culture with a meaning which speaks to human needs and intuitions at a level deeper than the cultural differences? Do cultural differences prevent the impact, or even blunt the edge, of teachings like 'everyone who exalts himself will be humbled, but he who humbles himself will be exalted' (Luke 18: 14), or 'unless a grain of wheat falls into the earth and dies, it remains alone; but if it dies it bears much fruit' (John 12: 24) or 'what does it profit a man, to gain the whole world and forfeit hs life?' (Mark 8: 36). Even teaching which requires some technical knowledge for its understanding may evoke some recurrent moral issue. I have for instance never myself preached about the saying of Jesus concerning Corban (Mark 7: 11), as I am sure I would get the Jewish technicalities wrong; but does not that episode illustrate a timeless principle, that it is wrong to use a religious duty so as to evade a paramount moral obligation? Instances could be multiplied of the co-existence of passing technicality and lasting principle.

Second, the examples of the reading of modern notions into the ancient writings which Nineham gives are not wholly convincing. What is called 'realized eschatology' is not a 'modern hybrid'. So far from being either modern or hybrid it does no more than describe the belief that God is both here and is to come, a belief attested in the gospel

tradition and seldom absent from the Christian consciousness both in the apostolic age and subsequently.
Already the Kingdom is here, yet the Christians pray for
its coming. Already the Christians have life hid with
Christ in God, yet they look forward to being with him
and seeing him as he is. Some words of Bishop B. C.
Butler may be quoted:

The doctrine of the two-fold coming of the Kingdom of God lies
at the very heart of the Christian religion considered as a
historical phenomenon. It is the same doctrine as the classical
Christian doctrine of the state of grace as a real but mysterious
anticipation of the blessed in heaven in the enjoyment of the
beatific vision. It is this doctrine which distinguishes
Christianity from Judaism as a historical phenomenon.[2]

Nor is the modern expository treatment of the theme of
sacrifice a matter of either accepting crude ancient ideas or
else modernizing and smoothing them out. There is
already in the Old Testament a glimpse of the idea that
true sacrifice is that of an obedient will and a contrite
heart, and in the New Testament the idea of sacrifice is
seen to be sublimated by its association with Christ, so
that it is interpreted in the light of him rather than he in
the light of it. The modern expositor is able to accept the
crudity of the primitive ideas, to see below their surface
and to trace the process of a transformation already begun
in the apostolic age. That there is the peril of a superficial
modernizing is true enough, but some of the scholars and
teachers mentioned by Nineham have been more success-
ful in avoiding the peril than he acknowledges. This
theme will be discussed further in Chapter 6 of this book.

Third, there is in the teaching of the prophets and still
more in the teaching ascribed to Jesus a message which
while uttered *within* a particular culture is also uttered

*against* it and from *beyond* it. Here is one example: the prophet Micah in Chapter 6 vigorously attacks the religious practice of his time.

> Hear what the LORD says:
> Arise, plead your case before the mountains,
> and let the hills hear your voice,
> Hear, you mountains, the controversy of the LORD,
> And you enduring foundations of the earth;
> For the LORD has a controversy with his people,
> and he will contend with Israel.

He goes on to denounce the people for ingratitude to God for his goodness in the past, and for thinking that he is pleased when they bring to him burnt offerings, thousands of rams and rivers of oil, for:

> He has showed you, O man, what is good;
> and what does the LORD require of you
> but to do justice, and to love kindness,
> and to walk humbly with your God?

No barriers of cultural relativity prevent these words from speaking to those of every age who try to buy God's favour and ignore God's ethical demands, here described in a historical context in words of universal relevance. The prophet speaks to the culture from beyond it, for God has inspired him so to speak. As P. T. Forsyth wrote in his great work *Positive Preaching and Modern Mind*, the biblical message can sometimes speak to the 'moral condition of the total perennial human soul'.[3]

When we pass from the prophets to our Lord, the beyond factor appears in sayings ascribed to him. Certainly our Lord lived and taught within a culture, and it is not for us to belittle the Jewishness of Jesus as a man of first century Palestine, yet a flat one-dimensional view cannot do justice to him. Nineham rightly quotes Schweitzer on the futility of understanding Jesus, a first century Jew, as if he were a twentieth century German teacher. But while he quotes Schweitzer's warning that Jesus is a stranger to our own time he omits to quote his equally significant warning that Jesus was a stranger to his own time also.[4] It is this transcendental factor which is ignored, and religious insight can know, as rationalism cannot, that it is by being a stranger to every age that Jesus can be wonderfully near to any age. To quote Forsyth once again 'the eternal world from which Christ came is contemporary with every age'.[5]

It seems that two misconceptions can bring confusion into the problem of the pastness of the past. The one concerns the nature of the Christian Church. The Church is not merely a series of generations of Christians, each encased in its own setting of time and culture. It is rather a community of experience reaching across the generations so that the language of symbolism which it uses can evoke the past in a way which strikes a chord in the experience of the present. The other misconception is to understand the relation between the past and the present in predominantly cerebral terms, for the question is not only whether certain ideas of the past can fit the intellectual outlook of the present, but whether the past can speak to us now as human beings with our sin and our guilt, our hopes and our fears.[6]

No doubt it was because the Christian message spoke to the conscience and the intuitions as well as to the mind that there could be an underlying unity of Christian faith and religion in the apostolic age amidst the many different cultural settings in which the Christians found themselves. It is often pointed out how different were the

presentations of the Christian faith seen in the early
Palestinian Christianity, in the stages of St. Paul's
thought and teaching, in the various gospel traditions and
in the Epistle to the Hebrews and in the Johannine
writings. Yet there was one Christ and one belief that he
was alive; there was one Holy Spirit; there was one
conviction that the death of Jesus had happened for
mankind's salvation, and all Christians shared in the
power to face the world with confident faith in the
sovereignty of God. Unity of Christian faith and religion
could exist amidst the variety of cultural and intellectual
expressions, and what happens between the different
cultural settings in one period of history can also happen
between the settings of different generations. At the
present time I know more than one Christian priest who
has been able to present the Christian faith both in a
sophisticated western setting and also in primitive tribal
settings in another continent. Despite theories to the
contrary, *cor ad cor loquitur*.

There is however a more radical question to be faced.
Scientific revolution in the last century has brought about
immense changes in the understanding and the presentation of the Christian faith. The acceptance by Christian
teachers of the historical criticism of the Bible and of the
findings of evolutionary biology have radically altered the
presentation of biblical revelation and of the doctrine of
creation and the fall of man. Amidst such changes is there
an identity of Christian faith between the early days of
Christianity and the present age? I believe that when the
radical changes in interpretation and presentation have
been fully admitted it remains that there is an underlying
identity in the faith that is believed and in the gospel that
is preached.

Certainly no change in Christianity has been greater

than the new understanding of creation and the fall of man, and the preacher today is likely to be saying things which would have startled and shocked his predecessors of a few generations ago. Can it still be claimed that it is the same gospel which is being preached?

Creation is not understood today as a divine activity completed in six days as the book of Genesis describes it, or a process with the climax of the special creation of mankind's two first parents in the Garden of Eden. Rather is creation understood as the continuing movement of a divine activity through nature in many stages leading up to the emergence of the human race. Further, it may be right to think of creation as not yet complete and of man as called to the adventure of sharing in God's creative work as his adopted son and fellow worker, while retaining his creatureliness and utter dependence upon the creator. The Christian preacher today will draw out the nature of God's creation as a continuing process, while still witnessing to the creator–creature relationship whereby man is frail and dependent.

So too there is a radical reappraisal of the fall of man, so radical that the use of the word 'fall' is questionable. No longer is it thought that mankind's first parents collapsed from a state of innocence, bringing pain and death as a punishment. Rather does man emerge in the evolutionary process childlike and yet with the dawning of conscience and moral responsibility. But while man's moral and spiritual progress has been a reality, so has a twist towards selfishness, pride and the rejection of the call of con-science, leading on to a collective state of sinful habit from which there can be deliverance only by the interventions of God's grace. The term 'fall' can thus denote not the act of a moment but a movement, a condition and a state of fallenness, while the term 'original sin' still denotes the liability to sin, now deep in society, which causes the individual's sinful choices. If our individual experience attests this understanding of the operation of sin, so does the history of successive civilizations. Moral and spiritual, as well as intellectual, achievements are followed by catastrophes of triumphalist pride, decadence, and false ideals. A world that chooses such courses becomes a world under judgement, describable in the psalmist's words, 'And he gave them their desire: and sent leanness withal into their soul' (Psalm 106: 15, *BCP*). Created in order to rule many of nature's processes while being himself under God's sovereignty, man in rejecting God's sovereignty has found himself subjected to processes which it is beyond his power to control.

Thus has the understanding of creation and the fall changed in the intellectual revolution in the modern world. Yet experience has shown that it is still possible for the Christian preacher to accept these changes and to present the essence of the biblical message concerning the relation of God, man and the world. Incredible as an historical figure, Adam stands as a symbol of man's privilege and man's catastrophe. There still stands the theme that God is creator, that man is made in God's likeness with immense power in relation to nature and the responsibility of using that power for God's glory. There still stands the intuition that man's sinful predicament is grim, in the abuse of nature and the perversion of civilization and in an impasse which is irremovable without God's costly deliverance. In our very different context Christianity may still draw from the Bible the essence of theism, with the gospel of the death and resurrection of the Christ of God as the climax.

Those who are striving to witness to the Christian message today in a variety of changing cultural contexts have much to learn from those who study the problems of cultural relativity, for the questions are real ones. But the experience of what is possible matters no less than *a priori* theory about what ought to be possible. And a deeper question is at stake. Is it possible for Almighty God to inspire people in one age to do and to say things which will speak to the conscience and the imagination of people in very different ages? If it is not possible, it is hard to see how either revelation or Christianity can have much meaning.

## Chapter Three

# JESUS AND HISTORY

### I

What do we know about the history of Jesus of Nazareth? And how do we know it? In my previous series of Hale Lectures in 1959, with the title *From Gore to Temple, an Era in Anglican Theology*, I discussed a period in which theology was marked by a strong emphasis upon history and by much historical confidence. Indeed through a large part of the nineteenth century as well as the earlier part of the present century some famous words of Mandel Creighton seem to apply. Creighton said in his inaugural lecture as Professor of Ecclesiastical History in the University of Cambridge in 1884, 'Theology has become historical, and has not required history to become theological.'

The era thus described by Creighton came about with the decline in the appeal to the Bible as an infallible historical source and with the application of historical science to the record of the life of Jesus and the origins of Christianity. Both in Germany and in England the investigation of the historical origins came to have a large part in the work of the theological schools, and it was assumed that historical research can be conducted without prejudice or presuppositions, and that when the historian has done his work he can pass the result to the theologian for its doctrinal interpretation. In England the great names of this era include Lightfoot at Cambridge and Hatch and Sanday at Oxford, and its style and method persisted through the first quarter of the present century.

The work of scholars along these lines had its impact upon the ways in which preachers and teachers expounded the Christian faith. Without necessarily changing the content of Christian doctrine many would expound that doctrine less in terms of a system and more in terms of the person of Jesus Christ as himself the way, the truth, and the life. Bishop Lightfoot's words are well known, 'Though the gospel is capable of doctrinal exposition, and though it is eminently fertile in moral results, yet its substance is neither a dogmatic system nor an ethical code, but a person and a life.'[1]

Yet while scholars believed the life of Jesus to be knowable there was much variety in their view of the content of that life as disclosed by their historical studies. Different scholars tended to reach different conclusions about the history, each of them sure that his own results were scientific. There was the Jesus of History school, also known by the name Liberal Protestant, who held that the real Jesus was an ethical teacher who proclaimed the Kingdom of God, and that the messianic and supernatural elements in the gospels were unhistorical accretions imported by the early Church. In contrast there came in the early years of the present century the apocalyptic interpretation of the ministry of Jesus. It was contended by Weiss, Loisy and Schweitzer that the real Jesus was not the teacher of an ethical Kingdom of God to be realized in the course of this world but the proclaimer of the imminent end of the world, his ethical teaching being for the briefest interlude of months or weeks before the end came. In England especially there were also scholars who reached more conservative conclusions. In my early days as a student half a century ago, F. C. Burkitt was still maintaining that St. Mark's Gospel provided St. Peter's own reliable reminiscences of his days with Jesus in

Galilee and his own witness to the teaching, claims and miracles. Much influence was exerted at Cambridge and elsewhere by Edwyn Clement Hoskyns who used the prevailing literary criticisms of the Gospels to argue that the messianic claims of Jesus were present in every stratum of the traditions and there was therefore a true continuity between the mission of Jesus and the subsequent christology of the Church.[2]

Amidst this variety of historical conclusion it was however usually common ground that the history of Jesus was discoverable by unbiased historical inquiry. Distinction was made between elements in the tradition which were pure reminiscences and elements which were theological interpretation. But before the present century was a third of the way through its course this historical era in theology was beginning to pass away in face of a growing realization that history and interpretation cannot be so rigidly separated.

What then had become of Creighton's famous claim that 'theology has become historical'? Here is the verdict of one of Creighton's successors in the Chair of Ecclesiastical History at Cambridge. Dr. Norman Sykes in his own inaugural lecture in 1946 said this: 'The contemporary vogue in theological study is not wholly favourable to the historical method . . . The dominant claims proceed from an aggressively dogmatic theological system which is apt to show impatience of both the slow process and the modest results of the historical method.'[3] This is indeed a long way from the era described by Creighton and pursued into the present century by Burkitt and Streeter and others.

No doubt Norman Sykes was immediately referring to what is called the Barthian or neo-orthodox trend in theology which was powerful still in the nineteen forties, a trend in which the historical investigation of the apostolic age was somewhat irrelevant to the word of biblical revelation. But there were other factors within the large change of climate concerning history and theology. One factor had been the realization that in Christian apologetics too much weight had been placed upon the history, and the appeal to history needs to be supplemented by an appeal to Christian experience. Another factor was that the separation between history and presuppositions or between fact and interpretation seemed to be less and less tenable. More specifically, the new methods in New Testament study represented by Form Criticism and Redaction Criticism had much effect upon the understanding of the Gospels. All these factors had their part in the changed scene which Norman Sykes's words reflect.

How have Form Criticism and Redaction Criticism affected the historical understanding of the Gospels and the material available to the Christian preacher in his presentation of Christ and the living past?

Form Criticism studies the oral tradition of the deeds and sayings of Jesus in the decades before the Gospels were written, and shows the process whereby the Gospels were compiled from these oral traditions. It sees the episodes in the Gospels not as biographical reminiscences but as stories about Jesus told in the early Church in the context of the Church's post-resurrection faith and devotion and its didactic and liturgical needs. Jesus who fed the crowd in Galilee is now feeding the Christians every Lord's day with the bread of his own risen life. Jesus who stilled the storm on the lake of Galilee is present to still the storms which confront the Church in its mission in the world. Thus the Gospels come to be seen less as reminiscences than as testimony to Jesus as he has come to be believed and preached in the post-resurrection communities.

Redaction Criticism sets out to study the evangelists themselves in their modes, methods, and creative artistry, and sees each evangelist less as a compiler from sources than as the painter of an interpretative portrait, or as a writer who blends together fact, symbol and story-telling, so as to present what Jesus has come to mean to more than one generation of believers. The artistry of the evangelists may include a process akin to Jewish Midrash or extended commentary on Jesus's teaching. Here indeed is a kind of presentation of the living past very different from what was understood in the earlier phase of historical study. The past of Jesus is seen less as the past of factual biography than as a past that is known from its power to create a faith and a literature.

If these methods are followed, where does the quest of history now stand? In particular, how may the Christian preacher now use the Gospel material in expounding Jesus? Here is the answer given by one who is both a scientific critical scholar and one with a concern for the preacher's task. Canon John Fenton wrote:

Biblical criticism is the preacher's best friend. It directs his attention to what he should say, and does not allow him to say what he should not. It shuts the door on a kind of preaching that is merely historical reconstruction and moralizing thereon and demands of the preacher that he uses the text in the only way that is left — testimony. New Testament criticism has led us to see that the subject of the texts, whether they are Gospels, Acts, Epistles or Apocalypse, is about the risen Lord who is present with the congregations.[4]

This is a powerful statement of the view expressed. No longer regarded as memoirs of the ministry and teaching of Jesus the Gospels are to be seen as expositions of what Jesus had come to mean to the Church in the decades after the resurrection. How far, however, is this a complete or final understanding of the relation of the books of the New Testament to the history of Jesus? Is it right for the preacher to abandon all concern about what Jesus actually may have said and done in the days before the crucifixion?

## II

The centrality of the resurrection for the faith, the experience and the preaching of the Christians of the first century will be apparent to every reader of the epistles. But it is necessary to set out the different aspects of the resurrection faith, and to ask how they are related to history. Two factors are specially apparent. There is the belief in the continuing presence of Jesus as one who is alive. There is the happening whereby Jesus was brought from death to life.

Jesus was alive. St. Paul had no doubt of this, and he assumed that the Christians to whom he wrote had no doubt of this. Many aspects of the Christian life presuppose that Jesus is living and present. The affirmation 'Jesus is Lord' tells of allegiance to one who has a contemporary power. The recurring phrases 'Christ in me', 'Christ in you' imply the same. So does the celebration of the Eucharist as a participation in the body and in the blood of Jesus. So too does the description of the Christians as the body of Christ in union with whom the members grew into the fullness of his manhood. The belief that Jesus is living is expressed in the simple words of the Epistle to the Hebrews, 'Jesus Christ [is] the same yesterday and today and for ever' (Hebrews 13: 8), and in the beautiful words of the first Epistle of Peter, 'Without having seen him you love him; though you do not now see him you believe in him and rejoice with unutterable and exalted joy' (1 Peter 1: 8).

Besides the language about Jesus being alive, there are the references to the act whereby he was raised. With the exception of one single passage, John 10: 17–18, the language used in the New Testament is never about Jesus rising and always about Jesus being raised. The raising is God's act. Indeed it is God's *mighty* act, an act that brings salvation (Romans 10: 9), and characterizes the God in whom Christians believe. Thus to be a Christian is to 'believe in him that raised from the dead Jesus our Lord' (Romans 4: 24), and the Christians have confidence in God who 'raised him from the dead and gave him glory, so that your faith and hope are in God' (1 Peter 1: 21).

Something happened. The death of Jesus by crucifixion had shattered the hope which his ministry had created and made ludicrous the claim that the Kingdom of God was here. But a little later the apostles were confidently proclaiming not only that Jesus was alive but that they were sure that the crucifixion of Jesus, so far from being an ignominious thing, belonged to the divine purpose and was itself the way of salvation. There followed the experience, belief and preaching of the apostolic age. Was there an event which created the new order and what was its character?

There is the traditional view that Jesus was raised from the tomb on the third day after the crucifixion. Narratives about the empty tomb are found in the four Gospels. But it appears that the tradition is far earlier than the Gospels. In his account in 1 Corinthians 15 of the tradition which he had received St. Paul writes, 'that Christ died for our sins in accordance with the scriptures, that he was buried, that he was raised on the third day in accordance with the scriptures, and that he appeared to Cephas, then to the twelve.' The language seems to imply the empty tomb. On this understanding both the empty tomb and the appearances of Jesus are properly parts of history, but it has been urged that the resurrection itself being beyond human scrutiny cannot properly be described as history. It was an action of God indescribable in historical terms yet made credible by known historical results. For my own part I find no reason to abandon the traditional view that the body was raised from the tomb, believing it to be congruous with the historical evidence, the understanding of the resurrection in the New Testament generally, and a rational view of divine revelation. This last aspect has been strongly presented by T. F. Torrance in his work *Space, Time and Resurrection.*

Other contemporary scholars however are doubtful about the evidence concerning the empty tomb, and while they believe that the resurrection was a mighty act of God enabling Jesus to be alive with a powerful impact upon the disciples, they are uncertain what precisely this act of God was. Such a view, while it differs with elements in the New Testament, is at one with the emphasis upon the resurrection as being not only a continuing life but a divine action.

Yet another view has come into prominence. It is the view that it is misleading to postulate any particular divine action or event. The disciples had been utterly at a loss after the crucifixion, but now there comes to them the conviction that the Jesus whom they had known before his death has indestructible authority, significance, and indeed living presence for all future time. This view might be described as Jesus rising in the faith of the disciples. It is sometimes linked with Bultmann's theory of 'faith event', and sometimes with other philosophical or psychological presuppositions. While this view is some distance away from a good many elements in the New Testament testimony and understanding, it would seem to ascribe to the pre-crucifixion life of Jesus dynamic power and significance. We have then the paradox that a view which allows nothing to a particular resurrection history yet ascribes great historical weight to Jesus of Nazareth who evoked such faith from the disciples. One is moved to adapt Horace's famous words about nature and say 'Drive out history with a pitchfork, she goes on coming back.'

The upshot seems to be this. In all the variety of views about the resurrection which I have been describing it seems to be common ground that the apostles were convinced that Jesus was alive with a continuing impact upon them, and that they were right in being so convinced. Furthermore, the primitive preaching and the Pauline, Petrine and Johannine writings concur in their certainty that there was a *happening* which was the effective cause of the faith in the living Jesus.[5]

It is perhaps in this context of Jesus and the post-resurrection Church that we may consider a view of the historical question which has been prominent in the last few years. It is the view of Dr. John Knox that it is necessary to see the event of Jesus not as antecedent to the event of the Church but as one event with the origin of the Church. We cannot, he says, know the first apart from the second.

Scepticism concerning what can be known about the so-called historical Jesus has been widely current in the Church for a generation or more . . . This scepticism is bound to persist as long as men's minds are free; the grounds for it are too extensive and too real. But the more disturbing doubt is equally inevitable and has been just as widely felt: can our faith, can our whole religious position, be depending in any vital way upon historical facts so meagre and so uncertain . . . We need to see the meaning of the Church with our minds and to express it in our hearts. If God acted in history, as we affirm he did, he acted to bring this social unity into being. The historical event to which all distinctively Christian faith returns, is not an event in the Church or in any sense or degree prior to it, but is the coming into existence of the Church itself . . . Since we actually know this action of God only in the Church, is it not simplest to identify the event with the birth of the Church? . . . The event itself was nothing other than the coming into existence of the Church.[6]

Now certainly it is only because of the Church that we know about Jesus. If the Church had not come into existence our knowledge of Jesus might be confined to the meagre references to him in pagan history and perhaps even those meagre references would not exist. But we must avoid a wrong inference which Dr. Knox's thesis seems to encourage. While it is from the Church alone that we know about Jesus, the Church existed in utter dependence upon a Jesus who had existed before it and had created it. The language of St. Paul affirms the utter dependence upon Jesus of the apostles and the Christian community. Without Jesus the Church could not be. Without the Church Jesus did exist as one who was rejected and crucified, and we know the event of his rejection and crucifixion. The lonely and rejected Jesus was there, before ever the Church was created. And the Church both by the nature of its dependence and by evidence in its own literature shows us the event of the rejected and crucified Jesus. We need not hesitate to say that the event of Jesus is distinguishable from the event of the Church.[7]

### III

So the witness of the books of the New Testament to the resurrection of Jesus and to the significance of his death is powerful indeed. Is it, however, true that they provide no significant testimony about the preceding life and teaching of the one who died and rose again?

We have seen how Form Criticism shifts the emphasis from where it had formerly been in the study of understanding of the Gospels, but the degree of historical scepticism amongst Form Critics has varied a good deal. Amongst the disciples of Rudolph Bultmann historical scepticism about the life of Jesus has often been considerable, partly through an assumption that the early Church was not interested in that life, and partly through the philosophical concept of the gospel as being the faith-event of the death of Jesus as preached and believed. Not all students of Form Criticism, however, have followed this extreme line. An example was C. H. Dodd in his discussion of the problems in his work *History and the Gospel*. There he argued for 'a method of criticism which promises a fresh approach to the problem of history'. He described this as 'a method which does not aim directly or in the main at establishing a residual of bare facts . . . The aim is rather to recover the purest and most original form of the tradition which inevitably includes both fact and interpretation.'[8] Pursuing this method Dodd claimed to provide not indeed a chronicled account of the ministry of Jesus but a set of known facts about the relation of Jesus to his contemporaries, to God, and to his own mission in the fulfilment of God's purpose. These relationships as he portrayed them include these elements: the search of Jesus for the outcasts of society; the loneliness of Jesus as separated from home and family; the conflict of Jesus with supernatural powers of evil; the identity of Jesus with the line between the old order and the new; the rôle of Jesus in the fulfilment of the Old Testament hopes; the bringing by Jesus of divine judgement on the nation. There indeed is some picture of Jesus widely attested in the traditions, containing fact and interpretation and providing a base for the subsequent growth of faith.[9]

In the main, however, the exponents of Form Criticism have tended to hold that we can know for certain very little about the life and words of Jesus, and the conclusions of C. H. Dodd would now be regarded by many as old-fashioned. Criteria are sought for deciding whether a saying of Jesus in the tradition is authentic or a product of the post-resurrection Church. Two criteria often used are those of *dissimilarity* and *coherence*. The criterion of dissimilarity means that if a saying is without parallel in the teaching of the early Church or in contemporary Jewish teaching then it is likely to be an authentic saying of Jesus. This seems indeed to be a reasonable contention. But the converse seems a good deal less reasonable: that if a saying is paralleled in the early Church or in Rabbinic teaching then authenticity must not be claimed for it. It is hard to doubt that this notion can lead to arbitrary judgements, for is it reasonable to suppose that language used in the early Church could not have been used by Jesus and that he might sometimes have been himself its creator? The other criterion, that of coherence, means that if a saying, otherwise a good candidate for authenticity, is congruous with other sayings thought to be authentic, then it should be admitted.

Not surprisingly the titles Lord, Son of God, Christ are most often regarded as unauthentic importations from the Church's teaching. Rather surprisingly the phrase 'son of man' in sayings of Jesus is often regarded as unauthentic, although it would seem to qualify by the criterion of dissimilarity, as it is not a phrase used in the apostolic preaching. As the researches of students of Form Criticism ebb and flow with no sign of finality, and with a long waiting list of candidates for the Ph.D. degree eager to continue them, is it a right course for the Christian preacher to conclude that amidst these uncertainties he has insufficient knowledge of the history of Jesus before the crucifixion for it to have a place within his preaching? I do not believe that integrity requires so negative an answer. When all has been said that can be said about the Gospels as evidence of the impact of the risen Jesus upon the Church, it is but common sense to ask what sort of person was this Jesus whose impact was so great that they went on writing about him? We need to ask whether amidst the literature of interpretation, devotion, Midrash and poetry, the impression of a real person is not there. Did the real person make the literature, or did the literature make the person? There are overwhelming reasons for thinking that it was the person who made the literature and that the literature reflects him.

First, we notice that there was a concern about the human Jesus of Nazareth in the early Church. The Church's preaching reflects this.[9] So do references to the life and words of Jesus within the Pauline letters in spite of their intense concentration upon the risen Lord. So too the writer of the Epistle to the Hebrews who has as his theme the heavenly priesthood of Jesus bids his readers contemplate the man Jesus in his temptations, his prayers, his strong crying and tears, his godly fear, his endurance and his faith. The Petrine Epistle also urges its readers to imitate the humility, patience and endurance of Jesus in his approach to the Passion.[10]

Next, it seems right not to discount the collective impression of those sayings of Jesus which Form

Criticism frequently does allow to be genuine, as well as the impression made upon readers of very different outlook by the Gospel traditions that *here is a person*. Here is a person, peeping through the pages of the Gospels; a person who speaks with immense authority amidst a continuing self-effacement, who shows both righteous anger and gentle compassion, who is one with the outcasts of society and searches for them, who is aware that divine judgement is falling on the nation, who knows that in his own mission the fulfilment of the promises is happening, who is absorbed in the theme of the Kingdom or sovereignty of God, who accepts a vocation to suffer and die without contradicting the theme of the sovereignty of God, who has an intimacy with the heavenly Father expressed in the unique prayer apostrophe *abba*. The traditions do not conceal the person who created them, nor does it suffice to say with Dr. John Knox that we know the event of Jesus and the event of the Church only as parts of one single event together, for our glimpse of the person of Jesus is that of a bewildering figure who preceded the response of faith through which the Church came into existence.

Furthermore, is it credible that the post-resurrection Church could have almost at once been preaching with conviction the messiahship of Jesus unless there had been some foundation laid in his own ministry before his death? The evidence suggests not indeed that Jesus invested himself with messianic claims and titles in a formal way, but that he so preached the Kingdom of God as to show that its inauguration was happening by his presence and his coming death.

Thus the disciples are blessed because they see and hear what kings and prophets had longed in vain to see and hear (Matthew 13: 16–17; Luke 10: 23–24), for something greater than Solomon, greater than Jonah is here (Matthew 12: 41–42; Luke 11: 32). Because Jesus is casting out devils by the finger of God, the Kingdom of heaven is present (Matthew 12: 28; Luke 11: 20). But Jesus is frustrated until he goes to his death (Luke 12: 49–50). The disciples are called to share in his death before they would share in his glory (Mark 8: 34–38). But his death will not be a defeat or a disaster, for it belongs to God's purpose (Mark 10: 45; 14: 21) and it will be the ground of a new covenant (Mark 14: 24). To the implied claims about his presence and his death there is added the implied claim about the last day when it is Jesus who will confront men and women in the judgement (Matthew 7: 22–23).

If Jesus acknowledged messiahship at the time of Peter's confession he immediately interpreted it by the predictions of his death, and if he accepted the designation when challenged by the high priest a few hours before his death he did so as one who was about to die. It was the mission of Jesus to proclaim the sovereignty of God and to die. The Father did the rest. In that union of divine sovereignty and the death of Jesus there is the foundation of Christian theology.

# Chapter Four

# JESUS AND GOD

Jesus did not claim deity for himself. He proclaimed the sovereignty of God, a sovereignty realized in and through his own mission; and he gave himself to death. It was hard for his followers to grasp how divine sovereignty and the death of Jesus went together, but it was the union of divine sovereignty and the death of Jesus which came to be the heart of Christian theism. Years later St. Paul was to tell the Christians in Philippi that the characteristic of being divine is not to grasp but to pour self out (Philippians 2: 6). Perhaps that is the key.

The story of the emergence of Christian theism is an exciting one, and it is the context within which christology emerged. In the development of belief concerning Jesus the Christian theism was the supreme issue. What sort of God is it whose sovereignty the death and resurrection of Jesus vindicates and embodies? We need to ask what are the significant phases of the story which begins with the early preaching of the apostles and reaches a climax in the doctrine of the cosmic Christ and the Incarnation.

We begin then with the early preaching of the apostles. It is often overlooked how far-reaching are the claims concerning Jesus and concerning the doctrine of God implied in this preaching. In his first letter to Corinth St. Paul reminds the Christians in Corinth of what he had preached when he first went there, and that this was not a peculiar preaching of his own, as the tradition had been handed down to him, presumably by those who had been apostles before him. It was 'that Christ died for our sins in accordance with the scriptures, that he was buried, that he was raised on the third day in accordance with the scriptures, and that he appeared . . .' (1 Corinthians 15: 3–5). What does this tradition say and imply?

The message is not only about Jesus. It is about the biblical theism which in Jesus had been finding fulfilment. The term 'Christ' implies one who fulfils the purpose of the God of Israel, and the phrase 'in accordance with the scriptures' implies the same fulfilment. It is a message about the God in whom the Jews had long believed and about the climax and goal of his activity in history. This climax, fulfilment, goal, is, staggering to say, the death by crucifixion of the Christ. Further, the death by crucifixion has some relation to 'our sins'. Whose sins are involved? It implies the sins of Paul and those to whom Paul preached at Corinth and at other places, the sins of the other apostles and those to whom they preached in any places whether Jews or pagans. Indeed, wherever the message is carried the implication is that it relates to the sins of the people. There is no need now to probe into the exact meaning of the preposition translated 'for', and indeed a variety of prepositions are used about this in the New Testament writings. Let it be noted only that the death of the Christ concerns the sins of men and women anywhere and everywhere, and a confrontation of judgement is clearly implied. This is a message about a universal significance in Jesus, and it is also a message about the God of the scriptures, his purpose and his vindication.

More still, the far-reaching impact of the death of Christ is possible because the message goes on to tell of his subsequent resurrection. It is by the presence and impact of the risen Christ that the message is preached with power, received with power and vindicates itself wherever the Christian mission extends.

Such was the faith of the early Christians, a faith which already ascribes far-reaching power and indeed sovereignty to the crucified and risen Jesus, and this is in the context of the theism of the Jews in their biblical writings. The converts to Christianity in many parts of the Graeco–Roman world are, through their acceptance of the crucified and risen Jesus as their Lord, being brought not into a mere Jesus cult but through Jesus into the biblical faith now both renewed and revolutionized.

Nonetheless it is a big step from this stage of belief to the doctrines of the cosmic status of the Christ and of the Incarnation which begin to appear in the later writings of the New Testament such as Colossians, Hebrews and the Fourth Gospel. How did this step come about? It seems important to note that there are *two* streams of development. The one is the stream of the deepened belief in God, in his sovereignty, compassion and self-giving. The other is the stream of belief specifically about the status of Jesus. It is in the confluence of these two streams that the doctrine moves.

(i) The early Christians had a deepened faith in God, in his compassion and sovereignty. The Epistles resound with outbursts of gratitude to God and trust in him, not least in the context of suffering and frustration. The closing verses of Romans 8, for instance, are a signal utterance of faith in the sovereignty of God in the face of suffering and calamities of every kind. Here the apostle looks all manner of calamities in the face and declares that in 'all these things we are more than conquerors through him who loved us' (v.37), and that nothing in the universe can separate us from the love of God in Christ Jesus our Lord. Primitive Christianity is a story of the biblical theism winning acceptance in the Graeco–Roman world, as a theism which is both as old as the prophets but also

deepened and indeed revolutionized by the Christians'
experience of Jesus. How has the new conviction of God's
compassion and sovereignty come about? It has come
about through the belief that in the life, death and
resurrection of Jesus God acted with powerful significance in relation to the world. God's mighty power was
manifested in the resurrection of Jesus. But, more than
that, God was at work in all the events in a divine
self-giving. God commends his own love to mankind in
that Christ died for them (Romans 5: 8). God was in
Christ reconciling the world to himself (2 Corinthians
5: 19). It is of the nature of deity not to grasp but to pour
self out (Philippians 2: 6–7). In both Pauline and
Johannine thought the 'giving' and 'the sending' of the
Son by the Father are described with suggestions of the
costliness of the giving and the sending (Romans 8: 31–
32; Colossians 2: 13; John 3: 16; I John 4: 9–10). Finally,
there is in the Fourth Gospel the concept of the divine
glory as the eternal self-giving love of the Father and
the Son signally revealed in the life and the death of
Jesus.

So there emerges a theism in which sovereignty and
self-giving are blended.

(ii) The other stream of development concerned the
interpretation of Jesus himself. In this connection there
has been much said of the titles, images, and concepts
which came to be used, and of their various cultural
settings. It seems important to ask what was the character
of the faith towards Jesus which caused the titles, images,
and concepts to be used.

Jesus was *Christ*. In a Jewish setting the word would
mean God's anointed one, the Messiah. Away from the
Jewish setting the word could easily lose that meaning and
come to be little more than a personal name for Jesus.

Jesus was *Lord*. The title goes back to Aramaic-speaking Christians (cf. 1 Corinthians 16: 2), and it need imply no more than a deep reverence. But in its Greek form the word came to express the sovereignty of Jesus as in the formula 'Jesus is Lord', and it specially denoted the power of the risen Jesus (cf. Romans 10: 9). Further, as 'the Lord' was the title of God in the Greek Old Testament its application to Jesus could suggest undertones of deity. The title 'Son of God' need not of itself be of high significance, for in Jewish circles it might mean no more than the Messiah or indeed the whole Israelite nation, and in popular Hellenism there were many sons of God, meaning inspired holy men. What became significant was the intimacy with which the title was used, suggesting how precious the Son was to the Father and how costly was the sending of him into the world and the giving of him to death.

Two other kinds of language, as distinct from actual titles, came to be used in connection with the role of Jesus Christ. There is the imagery of the divine wisdom as God's agent in creating and sustaining the world and making himself known to mankind, an imagery familiar in the book of Proverbs and the book of Wisdom. There is also the imagery of the gnostic myth of the divine saviour who descends from heaven to rescue the souls of mankind and then returns to the spiritual realm whence he came. Both these images when applied to Jesus imply for him a cosmic role in relation to God and the world. Concerning the gnostic myth it is however clear that while the imagery of descending and ascending as applied to Jesus may have this background both in St. Paul and in the Fourth Gospel, there is the most profound difference between the content of the gnostic myth and the Christian belief. The gnostic saviour rescues human spirits from a world of evil because it is material and from a bodily existence which is no less evil, whereas the Christian saviour is one who is made flesh in order to redeem the entire cosmos and the whole life of man, for 'the body is for the Lord'.

It seems however that what is most significant is not the titles in themselves but the faith towards God and towards Jesus which caused the titles to be used. Again and again the verb 'to believe' and the noun 'faith' are directed sometimes towards God as object and sometimes towards Jesus. Faith in God and faith in Jesus intermingle. It is striking also that almost casually there are applied to Jesus texts from the Greek Old Testament which had been descriptions of God. These facts seem of the utmost significance for the character of the developing Christian faith. Nonetheless it is still a considerable step to the doctrine of the cosmic Christ found in the later Pauline and the Johannine writings. How did this step come about? The evidence suggests that the movement of thought towards the cosmic status of Christ came about not by the use of pagan concepts in a syncretistic manner but by the Christians probing the implications of their faith towards God and towards Jesus. St. Paul seems to begin to use the cosmic language not as one who is consciously adopting a new theory but as one who is finding the words for what has already been his inarticulate belief.[1] The tremendous assertion in 1 Corinthians 8: 6 that 'there is one God, the Father, from whom are all things and for whom we exist, and one Lord, Jesus Christ, through whom are all things and through whom we exist' is in line with the no less tremendous linking of Jesus with the divine sovereignty at the end of Romans 8 and the description of Jesus as 'Lord both of the dead and of the living' in Romans 14: 9. Let me quote some words of C. F. D. Moule:

They experience Jesus himself as a dimension transcending the human and the temporal. It is not just that owing somehow to Jesus they found new life; it is that they discovered in Jesus himself alive and present a divine dimension such that he must always and eternally have existed in it.[2]

So the two streams of christology and renewed theism flow powerfully together in the faith and language of Christians in the apostolic age. Indeed it is hard to separate them. C. F. Evans wrote:

It may be concluded then that there is a convergent testimony in the New Testament that early Christian experience was in the first place theo-centric, in the sense that Christians claimed to have a direct relationship with God and to know his power, and that it was also christo-centric. This faith swung between faith in Christ and faith in God, and yet was felt to be one faith since the former always reinforces the latter.[3]

The reluctance of the apostolic writers to say precisely that Jesus is God is understandable against a deeply monotheistic background, but the striking thing is not that the passages identifying Jesus directly with God are few[4] but that there is the recurrence of an attitude towards Jesus which would verge upon idolatry unless Jesus is not only on the creature's side but also on the creator's side of the line which distinguishes creature and creator. It is in this context that the language about the cosmic Christ appears.

He who is one with God as the author of the new creation wrought by the gospel is one with God in a timeless relation. So there came, in different imagery in different writers, the thought of Christ's oneness with the creator. So St. Paul writes in the letter to the Colossians: 'He is the image of the invisible God, the first-born of all creation; for in him all things were created, in heaven and on earth . . . He is before all things, and in him all things hold together' (Colossians 1: 15–17). So too the author of the letter to the Hebrews writes: 'a Son, whom he appointed the heir of all things, through whom also he created the world' (Hebrews 1: 2). Finally there is the majestic language of the prologue in the Fourth Gospel:

In the beginning was the Word, and the Word was with God, and the Word was God. He was in the beginning with God; all things were made through him, and without him was not anything made that was made. In him was life, and the life was the light of men. . . . And the Word became flesh and dwelt among us, full of grace and truth; we have beheld his glory, glory as of the only Son from the Father (John 1: 1–4, 14–15).

Here in the Fourth Gospel is the union of theism and christology in depth and in simplicity. It involves the worship of Jesus as divine, as is seen in the words ascribed to St. Thomas after the resurrection, 'my Lord and my God' (John 20: 28). The union is expressed in the moving words in the discourse at the supper, 'believe in God, believe also in me' (John 14: 1), and its character is expressed in the concept of glory, for the glory of self-giving in the Passion of Jesus is one with the glory of deity before the world began. It is a mistake to use sayings of Jesus in the Fourth Gospel as proof-texts for the claims of Jesus in history, for the Fourth Gospel gives us the interpretation of Jesus, the flower of the doctrine rather than its root. The root of the doctrine is, however, not only in the apostolic preaching concerning the death and resurrection of Jesus, but earlier still in the union of divine sovereignty and the cross in Jesus's own mission. John is near to the root when his narrative shows often that the ministry of Jesus is moving towards his death: 'If I glorify myself, my glory is nothing' (John 8: 54).

It is not to be supposed that what we have called the doctrine of the cosmic Christ was the common property of all the Christian communities even in the later stages of the apostolic age, or that the particular imagery was universally used. What however seems clear is that behind the imagery is the union of faith in God and faith in Jesus, and the belief in the cosmic Christ was not confined to any one writer or school and had its roots in that twofold faith. Furthermore, the Trinitarian language about God appears as the expression of a threefold experience of God's activity. The God of Israel revealed himself in the saving work of Jesus, and the disciples' response was itself inspired by the indwelling Spirit whom Jesus had promised. My own special plea in this chapter has been that the understanding of the deity of Jesus is closely linked with the divine self-giving, and the death and the resurrection are the key to the origin and development of the doctrine.

Is it however credible that the Word was made flesh, that God became man, as the Johannine doctrine says? For my own part I would say that it is just credible, in the way that Christianity as a whole is just credible, in the light of two considerations.

The one consideration is the affinity between God and man, as man is created 'in God's own image after God's own likeness', an affinity which finds fulfilment in the closest union that is conceivable. God in becoming man reveals signally what it means for God to be God as man's creator, and man taken into union with the life of God shows the potentiality of what it means to be man.[5]

The other consideration is that if deity is characterized by self-giving, the self-giving of God will go beyond all the analogies of self-giving which we can imagine. Thus the question of the Incarnation is one with the question of what kind of God do we believe in. Christians have believed in a God who does not only send messengers and prophets to give mankind information about his power and goodness, but gives his own self to take upon himself the life of man and the agonies of a tormented world. Some words of Father R. M. Benson of Cowley are worth quoting:

If the Word of God is to intervene for the elevation, purification, vitalization of man it must be by entering into the essence of man's organism. The higher life which shall accomplish the divine will must clothe itself with the lower life which has by death become incapable of accepting the divine will. The law sufficeth not, spoken as it was to man, so the Word must speak not merely to man but in man. . . . It is impossible to invest man's feebleness with God's omnipotence. God's omnipotence must come and clothe itself with man's feebleness.[6]

Such is the divine way.

The Church's faith in God and in Jesus preceded the use of the varieties of imagery to express it, and these in turn preceded the use of philosophical categories to express it as happened in the language of the Nicene Creed. Through the centuries the phrases of worship came to have a big place in expressing the belief, as in the 'Gloria in excelsis' or the 'Te Deum' where 'We praise thee, O God' is linked with 'Thou art the King of glory, O Christ'. The Nicene formula that Christ is 'of one substance with the Father' expresses the belief that Christ who is as human as we are is as divine as the Father, and this language has shown a lasting power to express the truth intelligibly in many cultural settings. But new modes of expression have to be sought, and within the present century there have been notable instances of the unchanging faith in God in Christ finding expression in new modes of language. It is possible that future history will attach less importance to attempts which are made at the present time to dispense with the Incarnation from the Christian faith than to the attempts made by contemporary thinkers to express the Incarnation in new modes.

If however the doctrine is linked with the death and resurrection of Jesus in the way that we have suggested then the deity of Jesus must needs be understood radically in terms of the union of divine sovereignty and divine self-sacrifice. Teachers and preachers of Christian orthodoxy, in patristic, medieval, and modern times, have found it easier to dwell upon the deity of Jesus than to draw out the corresponding truth of divine self-giving. Too often amongst the ancient fathers this need was hampered by the linking of belief in Jesus with a view of God as static, remote, and impassible. It was the genius of Athanasius to understand the Incarnation as the giving by God of his own self to the created world for its re-creation, and some striking words of Gregory of Nyssa may be recalled:

That the omnipotence of the divine nature should have had strength to descend to the lowliness of humanity furnishes a more manifest proof of power than even the greatness and supernatural character of the miracles. . . . It is not the vastness of the heavens and the bright shining of the constellations, the order of the universe and the unbroken demonstration over all existence, that so manifestly displays the transcending power of the deity, as the condescension to the weakness of our nature, the way in which sublimity is seen in lowliness and yet the loftiness descends not.[7]

But what is at stake is not only the union of sovereignty and self-sacrifice in the doctrine of God in Christ, but the nature of our Christian act of faith. To believe in the Incarnation is to commit oneself to living-through-dying as the meaning of Christ, the true life for man and the way of God's sovereignty in the world.

## Chapter Five

# HISTORY AND SPIRITUALITY

### I

Through the centuries there has been the phenomenon known as the Christian experience or Christian spirituality. It has been marked by a dependence upon God's gracious activity and by a relationship to the person of Jesus. But how closely is the experience linked with the historical events of the Christian gospel and with the tradition concerning them? That these events initiated the Christian experience will probably not be questioned; but, once initiated, is the experience something which goes its own way through the centuries with little recourse to its origin, or is it something which derives its character and has the power of revival and growth through a recurring consciousness of the events which created it?

Within the religious experience of Christians certain characteristics recur. There is the distinctive type of experience described as mystical, not indeed confined to any one of the world's religions. And the significance of mystical experience within Christianity may perhaps lie not only in its character but in the context of religious life of which it is a part. There is the sense of the presence of God, a presence at once mysterious and tender, beyond and within, a sense which can so disturb preconceived ideas for it to be unlikely that it is no more than their projection or reflection. There is the realization of divine grace, as the power to implant ideals of conduct, to enable a striving beyond natural powers and to resist the onslaught of temptation. There is the liberation of the person from fear and hesitancy into joyful trust and courage, compassion and hope. These are some of the aspects of experience known in Christianity through the centuries. The fruit of such experience is not autonomous, self-sufficient virtue but a realization of freedom and creativity mingled with a humble and childlike dependence.

Within the stream of religious experience there have been the men and women whom it has been natural to describe as saints. Their characteristic has been a rare humility. The saint's virtues do not inflate him because he is humbled before God, who is their source, and he is ever conscious that he falls far short of the perfection which is his goal. But while his sins may be bitter, they do not cast him down, as the divine forgiveness both humbles and restores. Another characteristic is a sensitivity to the world's sorrows as of one who feels and cares and shares, blended with a kind of heavenly serenity as of one who is sorrowful yet always rejoicing. Such is the saint's experience of God, and our own experience of the phenomena of saintliness in our midst.

It is evident that within the stream of Christian experience there are many varieties ranging from the characteristics of the saints to a diffused sense of God somewhat vaguely related to the Christian tradition. Within this variety there may be those who would say only that God is very real to them and that they try to do his will. There are those with an intense realization of the divine fatherhood or the risen Jesus or the indwelling Holy Spirit. There are those whose temperament causes their religion to be of the once-born type, and there are those who know the ups and downs of a catastrophic conversion. We need to ask not only how wide may be the variety of experience somehow related to Christianity, but also what are the resources of continuity and power of recovery, and how these are related to the original Christian history.

## II

It may be useful to pause and recall a fascinating episode in theological history in which the appeal to experience assumes a new prominence in ways which have been influential up to the present day. It is the rise and fall of the Modernist Movement in the Roman Catholic Church. Let it be clear that I am using the word Modernism not in the broad sense of liberal trends in general but in reference to the specific movement of that name which was prominent in the early years of this century.

Around the turn from the nineteenth to the twentieth century the historical criticism of the Bible was making headway amongst some Roman Catholic scholars. Among these was the Abbé Loisy. Born in 1857, Loisy became Professor in the Institut Catholique in Paris in 1890, but he was dismissed three years later because his critical teaching about the Bible aroused suspicion. Becoming chaplain to a community of nuns he was able to continue his studies and the first fruits of these was shown to the world in the remarkable book *L'Évangile et l'église*, issued in 1902.

This book was remarkable for the dexterity with which the author conducted two arguments at once. On the one hand he set out to demolish the liberal Protestant interpretation of the Gospels recently expounded by Adolf Harnack in his classical work *Das Wesen des Christentums*, known to English readers in the translation *What is Christianity?* At the same time he strove by his own treatment of Christian origins to provide Roman Catholicism with what he believed to be a sounder kind of apologetic.

Harnack's view was that when the historical factors in

the Gospels are pruned away the actual mission of Jesus is found to be the proclamation of the Kingdom of God as the fatherhood of God and the brotherhood of man. On the basis of his own scientific criticism, Loisy argued that Harnack's thesis involved an arbitrary treatment of the records and that the actual message of Jesus was apocalyptic, other-worldly, supernatural, and pointed to the coming end of history and a new age. Furthermore, it is wrong to see the essence of Christianity in its beginnings; rather should we look to its growth, to the flower rather than the seed. In fact, so Loisy argued, there grew the Catholic Church, partly from biblical and partly from pagan roots, and there is a true affinity and continuity between the other-worldliness of the message of Jesus and the supernaturalism of the Catholic faith. But the appeal to experience is paramount — the experience of the Catholic Church in the making of saints and in the union of human lives to God through the sacraments. Thus Loisy held that his own thesis both undermined Liberal Protestantism on its own ground of critical study and at the same time provided Catholicism with a new and better historical defence.

If the initial characteristics of Catholic Modernism are seen in Loisy's work it was a movement which embraced a variety of trends, theological as well as historical; and a strain of pragmatist philosophy and immanentist theology came to be present. Another prominent Catholic Modernist was George Tyrrell, a convert from the Anglican Church who became a priest of the Jesuit Order. Less of a biblical scholar and more of an exponent of ideas, Tyrrell set forward Modernist ideas of religion and spirituality in some very attractive writings. Baron von Hügel sympathized warmly with the Modernists in their plea for the rights of biblical criticism, but he became suspicious of the philosophical tendencies apparent. Not surprisingly the Vatican did not at all appreciate the attempt to provide Catholicism with a new apologetic, and was hostile to both the methods and the conclusions. The blow fell in the condemnation of Modernism in the decree *Lamentabili* and in the encyclical *Pascendi Gregis* in 1907.

For our present purpose, however, the significance of Catholic Modernism lies in the emergence of a new theological approach which, condemned within the Roman Catholic Church, came to have continuing influence outside it, not least in Anglican circles. In particular there were Anglo-Catholics in the second decade of this century onwards who, dissatisfied with the concentration on the historical approach made by Bishop Gore and others, developed an argument from experience akin in some respects to the thought of Loisy and Tyrrell. The most notable work on these lines was *Belief and Practice* by Sir Will Spens, Tutor and subsequently Master of Corpus Christi College, Cambridge, published in 1915. Spens was a lay theologian trained in the natural sciences, and his book was a notable attempt to treat theology as an inductive science which begins with the data of experience and argues from them towards their creative cause. Describing the characteristics of Christian experience through the centuries Spens argues that the creative cause of the experience was not a Jesus on the lines of Liberal Protestantism or a diffused Incarnation, such as was canvassed in some theological circles at the time, but the event of the Incarnation as Christian tradition had understood it. Only such an origin can, he argues, account for the characteristics of Christian experience through the centuries. In one passage Spens asks whether a symbolic story of Incarnation rather than an event might be sufficient cause for the experience, but he draws back in the view that the experience postulates the *conviction* that the event had taken place.

I have dwelt upon the story of Catholic Modernism and its sequel in the ensuing decades because the issues concerning history and Christian spirituality were most distinctly posed within this movement. In the decades since *Belief and Practice* was written the appeal to experience has been far more prominent in Christian apologetics, sometimes as complementing the appeal to history and sometimes as supplanting it. Lately an extreme application of the Catholic Modernist method has appeared in attempts to combine Catholic piety and sacramental rite with scepticism concerning both the historical origin of Christianity and the pattern of Christian doctrine. While there have been some who can sustain this *tour de force*, the spiritual casualties amongst those who have followed this method can be numerous. Worship and spirituality may indeed tide over crises of faith, and the will to worship may express the quest for God while the mind wrestles with its doubts. But, as we shall see presently, the heart of Christian spirituality through the ages has been the response to the divine gift in Jesus. In Jesus the gift is given to us and in Jesus the response is made; and the Jesus is one who died and rose again.

### III

There are passages in the New Testament which seem to describe some recurring characteristics of Christian spirituality. One of these is in the fifth chapter of the Epistle to the Romans. St. Paul is writing to Christians whom he has probably never seen, and he says:

Therefore, since we are justified by faith, we have peace with God through our Lord Jesus Christ. Through him we have obtained access to this grace in which we stand and we rejoice in our hope of sharing the glory of God. More than that, we rejoice in our sufferings, knowing that suffering produces endurance, and endurance produces character, and character produces hope, and hope does not disappoint us, because God's love has been poured into our hearts through the Holy Spirit which has been given to us. While we were still weak, at the right time Christ died for the ungodly. Why, one will hardly die for a righteous man— though perhaps for a good man one will dare even to die. But God shows his love for us in that while we were yet sinners Christ died for us (Romans 5: 1–8).

Here indeed is a picture of what the Christians were experiencing: a new access to God, forgiveness, inner peace, joy even in the face of suffering, the facing of a stormy world with hope. How has this come about? It has come about by the shedding of God's love in their hearts when the Spirit was given to them. But what does the love of God mean? It means the love shown in the death of Jesus for the ungodly. It is by that historical reference that the experience is defined and understood. The history did not only initiate the experience, it perpetually defines its character and inspires its renewal.

That the relation between the events and the Christian life is not only one of temporal priorities and cause and effect, but is also one of continued interrelation is shown in many passages in the New Testament. A few instances may here suffice. St. Paul, writing to the Christians in Philippi about the nature of fellowship in the Holy Spirit, urges them to have among themselves the mind which was in Jesus, and this is the mind whereby he regarded divine prerogative not as something to be grasped but as an opportunity for the pouring out of self in the Incarnation

(Philippians 2: 5–6). In the next chapter St. Paul writes of his own Christian life: 'that I may know him and the power of his resurrection, and may share his sufferings, becoming like him in his death, that if possible I may attain the resurrection from the dead' (Philippians 3: 10, 11). The life in Christ, initiated by Christ's death and resurrection, includes a continuing union with both and a growing appropriation of both. The link between the events and the Christian life is not a peculiarly Pauline concept, for it is equally prominent in the Johannine writings. In the first Epistle of John there is the close link between the revelation of life in Jesus and the fellowship of the believers who with him walk in the light (cf. 1 John 1: 1–4; 4: 9–13). In the first Epistle of Peter too the exhortation to the way of patience and forbearance in the midst of suffering is linked with the forbearance and patience of Jesus as he faced suffering and death (1 Peter 2: 21–24).

Such indeed is the link between event and spirituality that it is possible to trace certain norms of Christian spirituality appearing in the apostolic writings. Here are some of the norms which are noticeable.

(i) Jesus Christ is a continuing point of reference for the Christian life. It is a life derived from him, lived in union with him, and moving towards him as the goal.

(ii) The Christian life is characterized by the facing of the world and its calamities with faith and hope, and the faith and hope are based upon the divine sovereignty revealed in the events of the gospel. The continuing impact of those events gives resilience to the faith and the hope.

(iii) Beside the faith in the divine sovereignty with which the Christians face the world there is the faith towards Jesus and the crucifixion which is the ground of man's justification. Justification by faith gives to the crucifixion a continuing place for the Christian life. Again and again in history Christians will echo St. Paul's words, 'the life I now live in the flesh I live by faith in the Son of God, who loved me and gave himself for me' (Galatians 2: 20).

(iv) Then there is the activity of the Holy Spirit in the Christian life, for the Holy Spirit enables Christians to say that Jesus is Lord and to pray 'Abba, Father'. He creates fellowship and liberates into joy. His power is derived from the cross and the resurrection of Jesus and it is his work to make the impact of those events continuous. The teaching of the Fourth Gospel that the work of the Holy Spirit turns upon the glorifying of Jesus in the Passion, while it is a Johannine doctrine, gives expression to an essential unity of these themes already present in the Christian tradition.

It seems therefore that in the apostolic age there are present themes concerning the Christian life which are rooted in the history and are so characteristically Christian that their recurrence through the subsequent centuries is not surprising. While Christian spirituality has shown a vast range of emphasis and diffusion, times of renewal and recovery have been times of conscious return to one or other of the primitive scriptural themes. Thus St. Francis and his followers were inspired by a realization of the cross as well as certain aspects of the earthly life of Jesus. The Reformers had recourse to the Pauline teaching on justification. The Methodist revival was alive with a variety of biblical themes and images. The Tractarians were moved by the Incarnation and the life of the Word made flesh. In every case there is emphasis upon the priority of God's grace to the human response to that grace.

It may therefore be asked whether the priority of God's grace and the subsequent response to it may not be realized many times in the Christian centuries without a necessary recourse to the original history. Here it must be said that what the grace of God in the events of the gospel does is not only to initiate a series of acts of grace in subsequent centuries, but also to create the redeemed society, the Holy Catholic Church, within which successive generations of Christians grow together in the life in Christ. The Church reaches across the centuries; and the generations are united in a worship which centres in the adoration of their common redeemer, and in a life derived from Jesus and having Jesus as its goal in the fulfilment of his body. This fellowship of Christians, uniting the epochs in history, reaches beyond history to paradise and to heaven. We join with the saints in heaven in a worship whose centre still is Jesus crucified and risen, whose glory is reflected in his saints. These events have created the Communion of Saints and are the heart of its present unity and joy.

The Christian life is the recapture of the true relation of man to the creator who made him in his own image after his own likeness. It is a relation which includes the sonship and partnership of those who grow to work together with God, mingled with a deepening dependence, creatureliness, and adoration. The power to enjoy immense God-given privileges as God's fellow-workers, and at the same time to retain and to grow in the humility of the creature is one of the crucial aspects of the Christian life. But the humility of the Christian is drawn from the humility of God himself in the Incarnation, a humility powerfully described in words of St. Augustine: 'So deep had human pride sunk us that only divine humility could raise us up' (Sermon 188). It is worthwhile

to quote some words of Baron von Hügel written to one
who thought it possible to separate Catholic sacramen-
talism from the historical Incarnation: 'I fail to make
sense of your frequentation of Holy Communion, even of
Benediction, unless at the bottom of your mind there is
the instinct stronger than that of mystical inclination that
God does dwell in and manifest himself by historical
happenings, here more than there, now more than
then . . . We reach at last an apex of spirituality which is
at bottom the deepest self-giving of God in Jesus Christ
in the manger and the cross.'[1]

## IV

'Things are different now.' That sentence expresses the
most stupendous and challenging of all the Christian
claims, the claim not only that the living past of Christ has
brought into the world the sanctifying powers of which we
have been thinking, but that somehow the world has
become different. God has done something to it. God has
brought it into a new relation to himself by taking upon
himself the burden of the world's agony. Is this idea of a
divine work accomplished really credible?

The Christians of the apostolic age clearly believed that
it was credible, with their language about a divine victory
over evil and the beginning of a new creation and the
dawning of a new age. Eastern Orthodox Christianity
dwells upon the resurrection as the beginning of the
re-creation of the cosmos, while the Western Christians
have more often dwelt upon the cross as the bringing of
the estranged world into a new relation to God. It seems
that experience shows that some of the depths of a
Christian relation to God are drawn from the conviction
that in his death on Calvary Jesus won a victory powerful

for all time. This aspect of doctrine and of spirituality was the theme of the Hale Lectures given by Dr. Leonard Hodgson in 1950 with the title *The Doctrine of the Atonement*. I mention this work of one of my predecessors partly for his luminous treatment of this theme but chiefly because of a moving illustration with which his lectures end.

Some fifteen years ago there died in a hospital in New York an elderly English woman who had long been sorely crippled in almost every joint by rheumatoid arthritis. She was only not bed-ridden in that she could be bodily lifted out of bed and propped up to sit in an invalid chair and read a book on a stand in front of her. In constant pain, unable to move head or arms, she could not look round to see who came into the room, and when she came to the bottom of the right-hand page of her book she had to wait till someone should come in to turn it over. Yet such was the spirit and sparkle of her conversation, the radiant brightness of her personality, that for those who came to see her those visits were among the brightest spots of their lives. To a priest who was privileged to hear her speak of the deep things of her experience she revealed one day the inner secret of it. So far as she knew, she said, her disease had come from a germ which she had picked up years before while travelling in South Africa. Vigorous and alert as she had been in body and mind, it had been a long time before she found inward peace. It had only come when she had learned to make a daily offering of her sufferings to the Lord who ever liveth to make intercession for us, asking him to accept it, to unite it with his passion and death upon the cross, and with his intercession for the land and peoples of South Africa.

She added a word of caution. 'Tell people', she said, 'that they must never try to make use of these sufferings in lifting people out of their troubles and up to God. That tears the soul in pieces, I know for I have tried. You must not reach sideways, as it were, and seek yourself to do the lifting up. You must always look upward to Christ and simply ask him to take what you have to offer, and ask him to make what use of it he will. That way alone comes peace.'

It was spoken with the quiet authority of one who knows, in the matter of fact tone of a scientist reporting on the result of a laboratory experiment. One became aware that one was listening to a mistress of the spiritual life, who in one sentence could convey more understanding of the Christian faith than can be expressed in seven lectures on Christian doctrine.[2]

That moving testimony which I have quoted is indeed paralleled in the experience of many, but I know of no example more convincing than this. The lecturer added these lines which tell most vividly of the seeing of human suffering in the light of the living past of Christ.

> Christ's triumph is no doubtful incident
> Of Palestinian rumour long ago
> But through all after-ages hath extent
> That men may it contemporaneous know
> Through present power and life which well it can bestow.

## Chapter Six

# CHRISTIAN SACRIFICE

The concept of sacrifice, derived from the ancient Jewish sacrifices described in the Old Testament, was very prominent in the New Testament writers for their understanding of the salvation wrought by Jesus Christ. Our Lord himself used the language of sacrifice when at the Last Supper he spoke to the disciples about the new covenant in his blood and instituted the Eucharist as the memorial, or the recalling, of his death. This concept means little in the modern world and the Christian teacher has again and again to paraphrase or to interpret it. But whenever we paraphrase or interpret we need to be sure that we have first gone as deeply as we can into the meaning of the concept in question. So in taking the Christian concept of sacrifice as my theme, I am inviting discussion both of a central Christian doctrine and of the problem of religious language and imagery in Christianity.

The word 'sacrifice' has come both in popular and in religious use to be sublimated in ways far from its original history. It is used of giving something up, of making some unselfish gesture, of losing one's life, or simply parting with something. One of my own teachers, Edwyn Clement Hoskyns, used to say that it would be a good thing if a bull could be sacrificed once a year in the College courtyard so as to bring home to all our senses what sacrifice really meant in the world in which Christianity began.

Now at the time of the coming of Christ sacrifices had been for centuries a familiar feature, whether in the form of the slaughtering of animals, or the offering of their life blood on the altar, or in the form of bringing the first fruits of many kinds of produce as a gift to the deity. Amongst the Jews a variety of forms of sacrifice found a place within the religion of Yahweh, the God of the covenant. And as the Jewish systems of sacrifice developed, a certain rationality about their meaning became apparent. They witnessed to a deep feeling that as man approaches God something desperate needs to be done on account of the estrangement of sin. Man cannot easily slip into the divine presence; man, as a sinner, cannot lightly approach the Holy God; hence the strange system of sacrifices. And the idea of offering something to God is therefore present, and when the animals have been slaughtered, the blood that represents their life is offered on the altar. Perhaps the offering of the life of an animal is in some half-conscious way felt to represent the offering of the life of the man bringing the sacrifice. But of that we are not quite sure. For all its ceremonial elaboration, the system could not conceal hints of an inner scepticism about its own validity. Thus, some of the Psalms contain instances of sacrifices being the expression of man's piety, of longing for God. 'I will go to the altar of God, to God my exceeding joy', and the psalmist who can thus speak was undoubtedly one for whom the ritual was the outward expression of a sincere religious relationship to his creator. But we also find in the Psalms that what God really requires is not sacrifice at all but moral obedience: Psalm 51, for instance, 'For thou hast no delight in sacrifice; were I to give thee a burnt offering, thou wouldst not be pleased. The sacrifice acceptable to God is a broken spirit; a broken and a contrite heart, O God, thou wilt not despise.' But while the religion of the prophets could sometimes see sacrifices as the expression of a truly inward worship, there were also times when the religion of the prophets did denounce the whole as irrelevant. No words ever uttered by a prophet could have been more awe-inspiring than the words of the prophet Micah (6: 6–8):

> With what shall I come before the LORD,
>    and bow myself before God on high?
> Shall I come before him with burnt offerings,
>    with calves a year old?
> Will the LORD be pleased with thousands of rams,
>    with ten thousands of rivers of oil?
> Shall I give my first-born for my transgression,
>    the fruit of my body for the sin of my soul?'
> He has showed you, O man, what is good;
>    and what does the LORD require of you
> but to do justice, and to love kindness,
>    and to walk humbly with your God?

Now from the first days of the Christian Church animal sacrifices had no place whatever within its life. But instead of them the Christians now spoke of Christ's own sacrifice as the ground of their new relation to God. They spoke also of the joyful privilege of Christians to offer themselves, their souls and bodies, as the sacrificial offering to God which is their spiritual worship (e.g. Romans 12: 1; Hebrews 13: 15). For Christ had fulfilled, abolished, superseded the old system not by attacking it or denouncing it but simply by replacing it by himself, his own life, death and resurrection; himself the true victim, himself the true priest. And while the contrast between the old order and the new order is alluded to by nearly all the New Testament writers, it was the anonymous writer of the Epistle to the Hebrews who drew out the contrast in its fullness. The old sacrifices were bulls and goats; Christ's sacrifice is that of his own life, his body, his will.

The old sacrifices had no real moral effect. Christ's sacrifice had a cleansing power and enables Christians to make a true approach, offering themselves in union with him. The old sacrifices were a series of pathetic repetitions year by year. Christ's sacrifice once for all opened the way for lives to be effectually consecrated to God. He sacrificed himself once in order that the sacrifice of Christian lives in and through him could continue for ever. This is the aspect of the matter on which we are going to dwell. Despite the radical break with the past, the Christians continued to use the sacrificial language and imagery in describing the mission and achievement of Jesus Christ. How are we to understand the Christian's use of this sacrificial imagery?

The first Christians were experiencing a wonderful deliverance from the dominance of sin into a new fellow-ship with God based on divine forgiveness, and this experience was for them linked with the death and resurrection of Jesus Christ. In expounding the meaning of this the apostolic writers likened him to a series of images drawn from the Old Testament. Let me recall these images. Each of them was familiar in its Old Testament setting; what is new is the likening of each of them to the mission and achievement of Christ.

(i) Jesus is the passover lamb (1 Corinthians 5: 7; 1 Peter 1: 19). Jesus did for the people of God whatever the passover lamb represented for the people of the old covenant.

(ii) Jesus is the sin offering. The image is of the offering made once a year when the high priest entered the holy of holies taking with him a sacrifice designed to cleanse the holy places and the community (Hebrews 9: 25; Romans 3: 21–26).

(iii) Jesus is like the scapegoat who carries away the sins

of the people into the uninhabited regions (1 Peter 2: 24; 2 Corinthians 5: 21).[1]

(iv) Jesus is the inaugural sacrifice, initiating the new covenant (Mark 14: 24; 1 Peter 1: 2; Hebrews 9: 19). This recalls the scene in Exodus 24 when, at the inauguration of the old covenant, sacrifices were offered and Moses dashed some of the blood over the people and some upon the altar.

(v) Jesus is the Lamb of God, who takes away the sin of the world (John 1: 29). Where does that image come from? It does not seem to correspond with any particular Old Testament image, as the passover lamb was not in fact regarded as taking away sin. Perhaps we have here a new complex Christian image in which several Jewish images are fused together in a composite picture of Christ as 'the Lamb of God'.

So we find this series of sacrificial pictures applied to Jesus Christ. He fulfils them all, supersedes them all; but all of them were used by the early Christians to convey the truth about the death and resurrection of Jesus for the world's salvation. How are we to understand the Christian use of these images?

There are several procedures which we might follow in trying to answer this question. We might for instance probe into the cult history and try to discover what each of the forms of sacrifice meant and stood for in the old Jewish religion, whether in early times or as the system came to be developed. And then we could define the work of Jesus in relation to that. I suggest to you that this would be an utterly misleading procedure, for — apart from the difficulty of discovering precisely the original meaning of the sacrifices — such a procedure would mean interpreting Jesus Christ by the Old Testament concepts when indeed he came himself to reinterpret the Old Testament by and through himself and not the reverse.

Let me suggest another procedure. It is to ask what is new and striking in the combination of these images in the Christian use and understanding of them. Perhaps in some of the new combinations and blendings of the images we see what is new and creative in the Christian doctrine. We shall ask in other words what was the effect upon these concepts of their association with one another and with Jesus Christ. There may be nothing remarkable about the images in themselves; but there are things strikingly remarkable about some of the uses made of them, and it is here that we may see the new and creative Christian phenomenon.

First, it is striking that Jesus is pictured both as the pure offering of the day of atonement and also as the sin-bearing scapegoat. It is indeed a remarkable combination. The offering on the day of atonement was meant to be pure and clean; as such alone was it acceptable to God. But the scapegoat, or the 'goat for Azazel', was a beast made unclean because the sins of the people were supposed to be put upon it, and all unclean he carried those sins far away to the uninhabited regions. Can Jesus Christ be, and do, both these things? Yes, he brings to the Father the pure and perfect offering of an utterly selfless and loving obedience and at the same time he takes on himself the burden of the world's sin, the total calamity of man's darkness, grief and estrangement. This is, in a way, the heart of the gospel. The Jesus who perfectly glorifies the Father enters the darkness of mankind's sinful situation in the dereliction of the Passion, going right into 'the uninhabited regions'. The key to this union of utterly different images is *agape*, the divine love in its Christian meaning. The love whereby Jesus makes his pure offering is the same love whereby he becomes one with sinners in their calamity. *Unus Christus, totus in Patre, totus in nostris.*

Second, a still more striking combination is the image of the sacrificial victim and an image right outside the sacrificial realm — the victorious king. Nothing is more significant in New Testament theology than the fusion of sacrifice and sovereignty both in the imagery of the lamb and the throne in the Apocalypse and in St. John's narration of the Passion.

Now there is a sense in which the combination is not novel. It is possible for the same person to be both a king and a priest, like the mysterious figure depicted in Psalm 110. But the functions and the occasions are different: to lead an army in battle as a victorious king is one thing, to offer sacrifices is another. But St. John in his story of the Passion brings out that Jesus is, in the one event, both the sacrificial victim likened to the passover lamb and the victorious king who reigns supreme. Remember how this blending of imagery runs through St. John's account of the Passion. Jesus dies about the time when the lambs were being slaughtered for the sacrifices of the passover festival. It was at the moment of the preparation of the passover that Pilate sentences Jesus to death, and several details in the scene recall the imagery of the passover sacrifice. Yes, Jesus is dying as sacrifice, Jesus is dying as victim, but in the self-same scene Jesus is a victorious king. 'Behold your king', says Pilate, and throughout the scene of Calvary Jesus is king indeed. He reigns from the cross, he cries in triumph 'It is finished'. Of his own will he surrenders his own spirit to the Father. The scene is a scene of kingship and majesty, while being at the same time a scene of sacrificial offering. And is this presentation of sacrifice and kingship in St. John merely dramatic pageantry? No, it is a presentation of the deeply religious concept which St. John draws out in his use of the term 'glory'. Glory speaks of divine power, majesty, sovereignty. But glory as interpreted by St. John in his Gospel is the glory of self-giving love, for it is in self-giving love that the divine majesty is supremely revealed, and it is by self-giving love that Christ conquers and reigns as king.

A third novelty in the Christian use of the sacrificial imagery is this. In the old covenant sacrifice was always something done from man in the Godward direction. So too in the new covenant sacrifice is what Jesus the son of man offers towards the Father, and the spiritual sacrifices of Christians are all sacrifices towards God. But strikingly there begins to appear the idea that while sacrifice is from man Godwards, it in some sense proceeds from God himself, from a divine self-giving which is the source of Christ's self-giving.

We find just a hint of this idea in 1 Peter 1: 19–20, where Jesus is spoken of as the lamb *fore-known* before the foundation of the world, the suggestion perhaps being that his sacrifice springs from some antecedent divine purpose. In Revelation 13: 8 Jesus is called the lamb *slain* before the foundation of the world, the suggestion perhaps being that his sacrifice springs from some characteristic existing from all eternity. I am reminded of a saying of P. T. Forsyth, 'There was a Calvary above which was the mother of it all (*The Person and Place of Jesus Christ*, p. 271). Then, in the Epistle to the Hebrews, there is the close relation between Christ's sonship and Christ's priesthood; he is son for ever and priest for ever, with the suggestion that while sacrifice is something which happens in time and history, it is the expression of an eternal characteristic. In Hebrews 9: 14 the phrase 'Christ who through the eternal Spirit offered himself without blemish to God' is hard to paraphrase exactly, but at least it suggests that when Christ offered himself in time and history it was in virtue of some eternal character or fitness. Christ did what it eternally behoves him to do. In St. Paul's writings there is nothing parallel to these concepts. But St. Paul is clear that in the death of Christ the love of God himself was active. God commends his own love towards us in that while we were yet sinners Christ died for us (Romans 5: 8), and God was in Christ reconciling the world to himself (2 Corinthians 5: 19).

I suggest that it is in these three revolutions in the Christian use of the familiar Jewish imagery that we find what is new and distinctive for Christianity. The blending of a Godward offering and an identification with man's sin and death shows the new meaning of love and holiness. The blending of sacrifice and kingship shows the Christian idea of divine glory. And the linking of sacrifice with God himself in eternity transforms the meaning of sacrifice. We do not interpret our Lord by the old images, rather do we see the old images revolutionized by their association with our Lord. This is how I understand the famous phrase of McLeod Campbell in his book *The Nature of the Atonement*, 1857, 'to see the Atonement in its own light'.

Do we now begin to see in outline a comprehensive Christian view of sacrifice? I suggest that we may begin to see it on these lines.

Ideally sacrifice is man's true response and relation to God his maker, and the reflection in man of God's own righteousness and love. Man is created in God's own image in order to offer himself with all his power to the Creator's glory in humble dependence upon him. St. Augustine thus describes sacrifice in its ideal form: 'Sacrifice is every deed that is done to the end that we may cleave to God in fellowship in relation to the good end by which we might become blessed' (*De Civitate Dei*, X.6). The concept of ideal sacrifice on these lines was followed by two eminent Anglican theologians. F. D. Maurice in his work *The Doctrine of Sacrifice* wrote, 'There is a ground of sacrifice in the divine nature; in that submission of the Son to the Father, that perfect unity of purpose, will, substance between them, whence the obedience and fellowship of all unfallen beings, the obedience and fellowship of all restored beings will be derived and by which they are sustained' (p. 109). Sacrifice, he adds, is not contingent upon sin, 'it is implied in the very original of the universe' (p. 118). And Henry Scott Holland in a series of addresses on sacrifice in *Logic and Life* wrote similarly, 'Even if no dividing line had ever severed man and God, still religion would consist in the joy of self-dedication, the joy of homage, the joy of offering, the joy of a sacrifice. There would still be the altar and still the priest; an altar of joy and gladness and thanksgiving and praise.'[2]

Whether an ideal concept of sacrifice was reflected faintly in some of the primitive ideas of sacrifice as communion-fellowship it would be hard to say. But man knows only the ideal of sacrifice darkened and distorted in a world of sin, suffering and death. So sacrifice takes on a sombre tone, and comes to be known in history as man's attempt to do something about sin's desperate estrangements. So it is that St. Thomas Aquinas, while repeating St. Augustine's definition of sacrifice, adds his own more sombre rider: 'sacrifice', he says, 'is every deed done towards the holiness of God for the purpose of placating him' (*Summa* 3, Q.48). And Holland in his exposition passes on from the chapter on the sacrifice of Innocence from which I have quoted, to a chapter on the sacrifice of the Fallen: 'sacrifice', he says, 'can only be now a recovery of allegiance from the sad and ruinous sense of finding oneself outside God . . . the sense of severance, the sense of death'. But the Christ comes, and in a chapter on the sacrifice of the man, Holland says that by his sin-bearing sacrifice Christ 'rededicates for man that very torment of death which he had suffered in penalty of sin'. And finally there is the sacrifice of the Redeemed, for 'Christ's sacrifice is no far away fact to be shown and gazed upon; it draws us also into itself'.[3]

I have followed Holland's thesis since it is, despite the Victorian rhetoric in some of its style, a deep and penetrating sketch of a pattern of sacrifice: the Ideal, the Fallen, the Christ, the Redeemed. To respond to Christ's sacrifice is to be drawn near to the act whereby he redeemed us, and also to recover through Christ the joyful meaning of our existence as God's creatures. There is a similar, if more modern, presentation of this theme by the Roman Catholic scholar Eugène Masure in his book *The Christian Sacrifice*.[4]

It will be apparent how close is Christ's sacrifice to the Eucharist, for there his sacrifice is present both in that aspect which is solitary and unshared and in that aspect in which the faithful participate, as in St. Augustine's words, 'This is the Christian sacrifice, the many become one body in Christ' (*De Civitate Dei*, X.20).

Do we not see in the figure of Christ the aspects of sacrifice all gathered into one and all being thus transformed? In him we see humanity in joyful communion with God, the living out of man's true life of sacrifice. In him we see no less the lonely sin-bearing and the sharing in man's death and estrangement, 'Himself bore our sins and carried our sorrows'. In him we see no less the perfect obedience of self-giving love conquering sin, the manifestation of true glory. Seen in isolation every one of these sacrificial images can mislead, just as seen in isolation every one of the historic theories of atonement may mislead. But seen as facets of one single mystery, seen as baptized into Christ, the images can all have significance. Calvary and Easter shed their own light, and in their light we see light.

In particular this is true of the imagery which concerns the impact of the cross upon human lives. In several of the New Testament writers there is the imagery, drawn directly from the old rites, of being 'sprinkled with the blood of Jesus Christ'. Interpreted in Christ's own light does not this imagery really mean that the self-offering or self-giving seen in Christ's obedience unto death is given to us by the indwelling of the Holy Spirit so that we make it our own, are filled with it and cleansed by it? Again, there is the Johannine imagery of the glory of Christ being given to the disciples, 'the glory which thou hast given me I have given to them' (John 17: 22). What does this mean except that the self-giving love in the Passion of our Lord is by the Holy Spirit brought within our lives to oust and replace our sinful self-centredness? If that be so, the inner meaning of the blood and the glory is not so very different. As so often the underlying unity of Christian doctrines is greater than the differences apparent on the surface.

The Christian teacher today finds the imagery of sacrifice remote indeed from the modern world. He must and he will paraphrase and interpret. But in doing so he will strive to be faithful to the depth, the unity, the mystery, the Christ-likeness of that which he is paraphrasing. Let him school himself in the way in which the old concepts were reinterpreted by the apostles in their witness to Christ; in the deep and costly apprehension of sacrifice by some of the greatest Christian teachers of all time; in the meaning of the concepts for Christian life and spirituality—and then he will be equipped to paraphrase without misrepresentation, to interpret without diluting. And however much new language is needed, and I am quite sure it is, let the Christian Church always conserve at the heart of its worship the words of our Saviour himself about the blood of the covenant, for no words ever uttered in history are more universally significant than these.

I wonder also whether the imagery in the Apocalypse of the lamb and the throne has outlived its significance? It is the union of sovereignty and sacrifice that is the heart of the Christian message. Is there in this world, dark, divided, bewildered, and bewildering any meaning, shape, purpose, clue, sovereignty? Our Christian answer is: Yes, there is meaning, shape, purpose, clue, sovereignty—and these are found in the death and resurrection of the Christ, in the way of living-through-dying. It is through such sacrificial love that God's sovereignty is known, and evil is already being overcome; and one day its victory will be complete. The lamb and the throne: here is the true way of life for man, and the unveiling of the heart of God.

Such indeed is the Christian message. We learn its meaning partly by sitting at the feet of the apostles of Christ and partly from our own sharing in the agony of the world in which we live. It is the message that in the life, death, and resurrection of Jesus Christ, God gives himself to mankind in utter self-giving love, sharing and bearing the world's calamity, so that in Christ and through Christ men and women may be freed to give themselves to God, to one another, and to the service of the world. But words alone will not suffice to bring this message home. It will be brought home to the world by a community of Christian people who live by it, joyfully sacrificial in their union with God in worship, in their union with one another in fellowship, and in their service of humanity. Where Christian people are themselves a sacrifice of praise the divine voice is heard, and the world may begin to respond to its own true meaning.

## Chapter Seven

# THE CHRISTIAN STORY TODAY

The Christian story continues to be told, and today it faces as many questions as at any time in the past. This book has discussed the recurring question whether what we have called the divine story, with the belief in the divine Jesus, is the true interpretation of Jesus. We saw how the divine story seems to have arisen not from a self-conscious importation from pagan mythology but from the blending of faith in God and faith in Jesus amongst the early Christians. We saw too how the belief in the deity of Jesus was blended with the belief in the divine self-giving. The story led on to the dogmas and definitions, and the Creed of Nicaea uses a single philosophical term to say that Jesus who is as human as we are is as divine as the Father. We cannot doubt that other words and images have been used and will be used to express this truth. There may too always be those who shrink from verbal definition while they are sure that their faith in God and their faith in Jesus are of one piece. So too there may always be those who are less happy with the language of definition than with the language of worship, in which the Holy Spirit 'together with the Father and the Son is worshipped and glorified.'

It is one thing to say that the belief in Jesus as divine and human may be expressed in new kinds of story, image, or definition. It is another thing to say that the Incarnation is a mistaken and dispensable concept. The language of those who call for reconstruction has sometimes been ambiguous between these two theses, and it is thus that confusion arises in contemporary discussion.[1] It will not be surprising if contemporary writers who argue that the

Incarnation is a dispensable concept may prove to have less of a lasting importance than some who are exploring new modes of expression of the traditional faith. I am thinking of such writers as D. M. Baillie in the recent past and Karl Rahner, Wolf Pannenberg and John Macquarrie amongst our contemporaries.[2]

Not surprisingly contemporary interpreters of christ-ology are eager to do full justice to the humanity of Jesus, for it has been all too possible for exponents of orthodoxy to fail to do this and indeed to suggest a kind of docetism. Thus it is a contemporary trend to explore christology from 'below' rather than from 'above'. It had been customary to ask how the divine Word can take upon himself full and complete humanity. The contemporary quest is rather to ask how human nature may be its truest self through a transcendental dimension so that perfect humanity is seen in the divine Christ. If both quests find an answer in the Word made flesh it is the latter quest which has now come into valuable prominence.

So too the emphasis upon the divine self-giving in Jesus brings into prominence again the question of God and suffering. If the rigid conception of divine impassibility seems impossible to follow, and if we find ourselves saying that God suffers, we need to speak carefully about the sense in which this is so. God, it seems, suffers in the sufferings of his creatures and children. But he suffers not as one who is frustrated and to be pitied but as one whose suffering is rooted in a love which is redeeming and triumphant. Important issues for contemporary theology are posed in Moltmann's book *The Crucified God*, and if his treatment of the questions is too subtle to be wholly convincing the questions are central for theology and christology today.

However, besides the theological interpretation of the

Christian story, there is the practical bearing of the story
for those who are perplexed by theism itself and find the
language both of theism and of christology difficult. Here
the believer must needs meet the perplexed questioner
with humble sensitivity. To the perplexed seeker after
God is the Christian belief in Jesus an added burden, or
may the person of Jesus be a road towards the intelligi-
bility of God in the way suggested by the words 'Believe in
God, believe also in me'? (John 14: 1).

In Dr. Baelz's Bampton Lectures for 1974 with the title
*The Forgotten Dream* we listen to an imaginary discussion
between a 'believer' whose faith is marked by sensitivity
to those who doubt and a 'half-believer' who approaches
the problem with reverence and a religious temper
without any rigid rationalism and yet is never quite able to
say *credo*. In this dialogue one feature struck me as being
very significant: the place where the paths of the believer
and the half-believer converge, so that for a time the two
are walking most nearly together, is the story of Jesus of
Nazareth.

What is this aspect of Jesus, where the believer is saying
something to which the half-believer warms, and the
half-believer uses accents very near to those of faith? It
concerns what is called the 'perspective of Jesus'.

He saw the world as God's world, and this with an immediacy
and intensity of vision that overshadowed all else, making the
distant one present, bringing God to earth . . . For Jesus the one
inseparable and ever-ruling fact of the world was the fact of God
himself, and that the recognition of this fact by man was a matter
of extreme urgency, a matter of life and death.

Such a fundamental perspective determined the orientation
of Jesus's whole life . . . Reflecting the indiscriminate love of
God he loved indiscriminately . . . He chose the way of sacrificial
love . . . He proclaimed the forgiveness of sins, he *was* the

forgiveness of sins. If the matter of Jesus's teaching and the manner of his living expressed the way of sacrificial love, so too did the encompassing of his dying. It was an extension of the mode of his life into the mode of his death. We may understand it first and foremost as the final and irrevocable statement of his chosen way of life. Life and death were of one piece in a single integrity of action and passion (pp. 73–75, 79).

Thus far does the half-believer go. He senses that God is made real in Jesus's description of him, a description translated into a sacrificial love with the cross as one piece with the life, the act of power and passion. Thus near the half-believer has come, and it is along a path of history. And now the believer speaks; he says that in what has so far been said we are not far from the 'resurrection faith', the divine vindication of sacrificial love, and we are not far from the Johannine picture of the cross as divine glory.

Thus Jesus's death becomes more than the statement of a man, written in blood and moulded by the forces of human integrity. It is also a statement of God, in which death is subsumed into life and despair gives place to hope (p. 82).

So the believer is speaking on the half-believer's ground. He goes on to say that for both of them, indeed for all, the response is to follow the way of living through dying. Only thus do we begin to know the doctrine. But the believer is able to go on to say that in Jesus we confront not only the way of life for man but something describable as 'the heart of things', 'the mystery', 'the Word of God'. If this imaginary dialogue represents, as I believe it does, the way in which the mind of faith and the mind of half-belief sometimes come very close, then need we be hesitant in thinking that there is in the story of Jesus a Word of God beyond boundaries of time and culture?

How does this belief in the Word of God in Jesus bear

upon the growing mutual awareness and reverence amongst the great religions of the world? Christians, Jews, Muslims, Hindus, Buddhists, are more aware of one another's religions than ever before, and we ask, how stands the particularity of the divine Word in Jesus?

It seems that the Johannine prologue gives a clue. The divine Word is active within the human race bringing illumination to minds and consciences. 'In him was life and the life was the light of men.' Within many religions the light is present, obscured as it may be by human perversities. It is for Christians to acknowledge the divine light wherever they are aware of it with an unselfconscious reverence while no less unselfconsciously believing that in Jesus there is the divine light in its perfection. Thus the Christian evangelist is called to a frightening unity of humility and assertion, and in that unity of humility and assertion the claim will be not for a 'system' or a 'religion' so much as for Christ himself. So it is that following the Johannine prologue both in its prelude and in its climax there are indeed evangelists who tell us that while they bring Christ to people of other faiths they may find that Christ is there already. Their message is the fullness of faith in a Christ who is the divine light already present.

So the Christian story stands, but the questionings about it never cease, and again and again it will be asked: what kind of story is this? That the story is inspired, Christians have believed through the centuries. But it is an immense gain wherever it is acknowledged that literal chronicle is not the only sphere for inspiration and that drama, symbol and poetry can be an inspired mode of revelation. If God is the God of earth and of heaven the story will tell both the facts of history describable in one way and God's own giving and loving describable in another. It was salutary when the historical rigour of what we have called the Creighton era was devoted to the origins of Christianity with the assurance that fact is here. It was salutary also when the limitations of that era disclosed themselves and there came less separation between fact and meaning, history and interpretation. It was salutary again when it was seen that the traditions about Jesus are less diary memoirs than testimony to the impact of Jesus as preached and believed. Yet behind the traditions there is, as we have seen, a knowable person who lived and talked and died, an event of Jesus before the event of the Church.

I must end with some words about the bearing of our theme upon the Church. If indeed we are right in thinking that the key to Christian theism and christology is the death and resurrection of the Messiah, the implications not only for the tasks of the Church but for the Church's essential meaning are profound. Forgive me if I lapse for a moment into autobiography and recall the first book that I ever wrote. It was written nearly forty-five years ago at Lincoln with the title *The Gospel and the Catholic Church*, and it was its theme that the nature of the Church was defined by the participation of the Christians in the death and resurrection of our Lord.

The study of the New Testament points to the death and resurrection of the Messiah as the central theme of the gospels and epistles, and shows that these events were intelligible only to those who shared in them by a more than metaphorical dying and rising again with Christ. It is the conviction of this book that in this dying and rising again the very meaning of the Church is found, and that the Church's outward order expresses this inward meaning by representing the dependence of the members upon the one body, wherein they die to self. The doctrine of the Church is thus found to be included within the

Christian's knowledge of Christ crucified. Before ever the apostles realized the full doctrine of the Incarnation or thought of the Church in terms of it, they knew the Church through knowing the Lord's death and resurrection. Thus while it is true that the Church is founded upon the Word-made-flesh, it is true only because the Word was identified with men right down to the point of death, and enabled men to find unity through a veritable death to self.

After developing this theme in relation to many aspects of the Church's life, I summed up near the end of the work with these words:

As he went to die Jesus embodied in his own flesh the whole meaning of the Church of God, for its baptism, its Eucharist, its order, the truth which it teaches to men, the unity which it offers to them, all these mean simply: he died and your life is hid with Christ in God.[3]

Reading these youthful words today I am astonished at their audacity, but through the experience of the years I believe them to be true not only as an academic conclusion but as a fact with which we live. The writing of the present work has reinforced for me their truth, for if the death and resurrection of Jesus have the part which is suggested for the meaning of the Christian theism, then the Church witnesses to God only by its baptism into the self-giving death of its Lord.

But the end is not there. If the end were there the truth might be unbearable, but the end is not there because the Christ of the living past is the one who died and rose and will come again, and the Church in belonging to his death and resurrection belongs to the promise of the future. My earlier book has been criticized, not least by myself, for missing the eschatological note as part of the Church's mission. In dwelling, rightly I think, upon the historical givenness of the Church as determining its structure and mission I spoke too little of the Church's growing into the plenitude of what it already is, and moving into the full realization of the truth and unity and holiness once given to it. Furthermore, as Moltmann has emphasized in his work *The Church in the Power of the Spirit*, the Christ into whose death and resurrection the Christians enter is the Christ who was from the beginning moving into the future with the power of his risen life. The historical givenness of the gospel and the Church matter supremely, as the gift is no less than the gift of God's own self. So too does the promise of the future, as Jesus is the same yesterday, today and for ever.[4]

As Christ is past, present and future, so also is the Church as it rejoices in the anticipation of the goal. 'It does not yet appear what we shall be, but we know that we shall be like him for we shall see him as he is.' Thus the Church lives in hope, and Christian hope rests not upon signs that things seem to be going well, but upon its faith in the divine sovereignty of sacrificial love. So we live in hope both of the goal of heaven and of the coming of the Kingdom of God in this world, and hope is stirred by the presence of the Holy Spirit who is in the Pauline teaching both the first fruits of the heavenly harvest and the promise of the heavenly treasure. So sharing in the grief of Jesus, the Church may also share in his joy. There is the joy of living in the awareness of another world, as we look to the things that are unseen. There is joy too in the present experience of the transfiguring of suffering of which we were thinking in an earlier chapter. When our grief becomes not ours alone but a grief shared with Jesus, then the joy of Jesus becomes ours.

So the Christian story continues to be told, and continues to be lived.

# NOTES

## CHAPTER ONE

1. There is general agreement that the extant text of the gospel of Mark ends at Mark 16: 8, 'they said nothing to anyone, for they were afraid'. While some scholars think that this is a mutilated text and that the book originally contained a further narrative, there are those who believe, or suspect, that Mark's Gospel ended at 16: 8 on a note of awe and bewilderment.

## CHAPTER TWO

1. D. E. Nineham, *New Testament Interpretation in a Historical Age*, 1976, p. 22.

2. B. C. Butler, *Searchings*, 1974, p. 221, in an essay entitled 'Collective Bias and the Gospels'.

3. P. T. Forsyth, *Positive Preaching and Modern Mind*, 1907, p. 30.

4. A. Schweitzer, *The Quest of the Historical Jesus* (English translation), 1910, pp. 397–401.

5. P. T. Forsyth, op. cit., p. 32.

6. This aspect is discussed by John Coventry SJ in a valuable essay on 'The Myth and the Method' in *Theology*, July 1978. He makes the point that 'It is a systematic error for the theologian to regard his task as simply an intelligible process of translation and evaluation that leaves out of account the believing community. They, and not the written words, are the primary focus of revelation, of faith, of the action of the Spirit, or inspiration.' He criticizes Dr. Nineham for 'a merely cerebral exercise which I regard as wrongheaded. It entirely bypasses the believing community that has existed in the intervening centuries and that exists today' (p. 260).

## CHAPTER THREE

1. J. B. Lightfoot, *The Epistle of St. Paul to the Philippians*, 1868, p. ix.

2. E. C. Hoskyns, *Essays Catholic and Critical*, 1926, in an essay 'The Christ of the Synoptic Gospels'.

3. N. Sykes, *The State of Ecclesiastical History*, 1946, p. 28.

4.   J. C. Fenton, *What About the New Testament?*, 1975, p. 185, in an essay on 'The Preacher and the Bible Today'.

5.   Amongst recent work on the resurrection N. Perrin, *The Resurrection Narratives, A New Approach*, 1977, discusses the purpose of each of the evangelists, W. Marxsen, *The Resurrection of Jesus of Nazareth* (English translation), 1970, considers the nature of the resurrection faith, and R. H. Fuller, *The Formation of the Resurrection Narratives*, 1971, examines the growth of the traditions behind the Gospels and their literary arrangement. G. W. H. Lampe and D. M. McKinnon, *The Resurrection: A Dialogue*, 1966, is a debate between the first two lines of interpretation I have discussed in the text. Don Cupitt, *Christ and the Hiddenness of God*, 1971, commends what I have called the 'non-event' concept of the resurrection. T. F. Torrance, *Space, Time and Resurrection*, 1972, sets the discussion in a wider context.

6.   For an acute criticism of John Knox's position see R. E. Barbour, *Traditio-Historical Criticism of the Gospels*, 1972.

7.   C. H. Dodd, *History of the Gospel*, 1938, p. 103.

8.   C. H. Dodd, op. cit., pp. 91–103.

9.   For this see G. N. Stanton, *Jesus of Nazareth in New Testament Preaching*, 1971.

10.   For interest in the life of Jesus shown in the Epistles see I Cor. 11: 23–26; Gal. 4: 4; I Cor. 7: 10, 9: 14; 2 Cor. 10: 1; Phil. 2: 7–8; Rom. 15: 2–3; Heb. 2: 10, 18; Heb. 4: 15, 5: 7, 12: 2–3, 13: 12, 20; I Pet. 2: 21–23.

## CHAPTER FOUR

1.   The movement of St. Paul's thought towards the cosmic role of Christ was discussed perceptively by J. M. Creed in *The Divinity of Jesus Christ*, 1938. Acknowledging that the development was considerable, Creed says, 'There is no sign of an abrupt transition in the development by which St. Paul and others reach these stupendous affirmations concerning Jesus Christ and his relation to the world. St. Paul's doctrine of a cosmic Christ seems to have asserted itself without inward strain . . . The great outburst with which the eighth chapter of the Romans ends still stops short of a personal statement that Christ is the agent in creation, but when St. Paul has proclaimed his persuasion that the role of God which is in Christ Jesus our Lord is the sovereign power to which all created things must yield place, the way has been opened for the belief that through Christ all created things came to be' (pp. 138–140).

2. C. F. D. Moule, *The Origin of Christology*, 1977, p. 138.

3. C. F. Evans, *Explorations in Theology*, 1977, p. 117, in a valuable essay 'Christology and Theology'.

4. The passages which bear upon an identification of Jesus and God are discussed by Raymond Brown in *Jesus God and Man*, 1967. He notes texts which seem contrary to the identification: Mark 10: 18; Mark 15: 34; Eph. 1: 17. He notes texts where the identification is doubtful on account of manuscript uncertainty: Gal. 2: 20; Acts 20: 28; John 1: 18, and where it is doubtful through the uncertainty of syntax: Col. 2: 2; 2 Thess. 1: 12; Titus 2: 13; 1 John 5: 20; Rom. 9: 5; 2 Pet. 1: 1. Texts where the identification is in no doubt are, he says, Heb. 1: 5–9; John 1: 1; John 20: 28.

5. On the plea that it is logically impossible for God to become man see Karl Rahner, *Foundations of Christian Faith* (English translation), 1976, pp. 212–228.

6. R. M. Benson, *The Way of Holiness*, pp. 35–6.

7. Gregory of Nyssa, *Oratio Catechetica Magna*, LXXV. Compare the same theme expressed by P. T. Forsyth in *The Person and Place of Jesus Christ*, 1909, p. 315, '. . . to appear and act as redeemer, to be born, suffer, and die, was a mightier act of Godhead than lay in all the creation, preservation and blessing of the world'.


## CHAPTER FIVE

1. Von Hügel, quoted in Mark Cropper, *Evelyn Underhill*, 1958, pp. 79–80.

2. L. Hodgson, *The Doctrine of the Atonement*, 1951, pp. 152–154.


## CHAPTER SIX

1. It is too much to say for certain that there is an identification of Jesus with the scapegoat in these passages. What however is clear is that Jesus is represented as being made one with the alienation of sinful humanity, cf. Gal. 3: 13, 'Christ . . . having become a curse for us'.

2. H. S. Holland, *Logic and Life*, 1883, p. 108.

3. For references to Holland see op. cit., pp. 114, 130, 142.

4. Eugène Masure, *The Christian Sacrifice* (English translation), 1944, cf. L. Bouyer, *Le Mystère Pascal*, 1945, and E. Schillebeeckx, *Christ the Sacrament of Encounter with God*, 1963.

## CHAPTER SEVEN

1.  An example of this confusion is seen in the volume of essays entitled *The Myth of God Incarnate*, ed. John Hick, 1977. While the authors complain that 'The traditional doctrine of the Incarnation has long been something of a shibboleth exempt from reasoned scrutiny' (p. xi), they ignore the most important critical and constructive treatment of that doctrine in recent times as by Baillie, Rahner, Pannenberg and Macquarrie, to mention only a few. While their aim is 'to release talk about God and about Jesus from confusion' they revive a series of long-familiar theses: that God was uniquely in Jesus but the traditional language no longer serves; that such uniqueness cannot be claimed in face of the variety of religions; that Jesus was the man of destiny or a prophet of the Kingdom of God and the Church's doctrine came in as a mistake; that we know too little about Jesus to sustain any of these theses.

2.  For valuable discussions on Christology, D. M. Baillie, *God was in Christ*, 1947, W. Pannenberg, *Jesus: God and Man* (English translation), 1968, J. Macquarrie, *Principles of Christian Theology*, new ed. 1977. The parts of Rahner's work, *Theological Explorations*, which bear upon Christology are Vol. 1, 149–200, Vol. 4, 101–120, Vol. 5, 157–192, Vol. 11, 185–229. See also the recent work *Foundations of Christian Faith* (English translation), 1970, chapters 5 and 6. As to the work of E. Schillebeeckx, the first volume of his massive *Jesus, an Exploration in Christology*, has just appeared in an English translation and I am not familiar with it. But there is great value in his older work, *Christ the Sacrament of Encounter with God*, which deals creatively with the person of Jesus Christ and the continuing life of the Church.

3.  A. M. Ramsey, *The Gospel and the Catholic Church*, 1936, revised edition 1956.

4.  For the recent revival of interest in the eschatological aspect of the Church see Y. Congar, *Christians in Dialogue* (English translation), 1966, *Decrees of the Vatican Council*, especially *Decree on the Church*, ch. 7, 'The eschatological and pilgrim church in union with the living Christ', J. Moltmann, *The Church in the Power of the Spirit* (English translation), 1975, L. J. Suenens and A. M. Ramsey, *The Future of the Christian Church*, 1970.

# INDEX OF NAMES

# INDEX OF SUBJECTS